Discovering Jesus in Genesis

Susan Hunt & Richie Hunt

CROSSWAY BOOKS • WHEATON, ILLINOIS

A DIVISION OF GOOD NEWS PUBLISHERS

Discovering Jesus in Genesis
Copyright © 2002 by Susan Hunt and Richie Hunt
Published by Crossway Books
a division of Good News Publishers
1300 Crescent Street
Wheaton, Illinois 60187

Cover design: Cindy Kiple
Cover illustration: Nancy Munger
First printing 2002
Printed in the United States of America

Scripture is taken from the *Holy Bible: English Standard Version*. Copyright © 2001
by Good News Publishers. Used by permission. All rights reserved.

Scripture designated NIV is taken from the *Holy Bible: New International Version*®. Copyright © 1973, 1978, 1984
by International Bible Society. Used by permission of Zondervan Publishing House. All rights reserved.
The "NIV" and "New International Version" trademarks are registered in the United States Patent and Trademark Office
by International Bible Society. Use of either trademark requires the permission of International Bible Society.

Scripture references marked NKJV are taken from the *New King James Version*.
Copyright © 1982, Thomas Nelson, Inc. Used by permission.

The author may be contacted at PCA Christian Education and Publications,
1700 N. Brown Road, Lawrenceville, GA 30043. Phone: 678-825-1100.

Library of Congress Cataloging-in-Publication Data
Hunt, Susan, 1940-
    Discovering Jesus in Genesis : covenant promises for covenant kids /
by Susan Hunt and Richie Hunt.
        p. cm.
    ISBN 1-58134-394-9 (alk. paper)
    1.Christian education—Home training. 2. Christian education—
Textbooks for children. 3. Bible—Textbooks. I. Hunt, Richie, 1967-
II. Title.
BV1590 .H86   2002
248.8'45—dc21   2002002479

LB		13	12	11	10	09	08	07	06	05	04	03	02
15	14	13	12	11	10	9	8	7	6	5	4	3	2	1

CROSSWAY BOOKS BY SUSAN HUNT AND RICHIE HUNT

Big Truths for Little Kids

Discovering Jesus in Genesis
Covenant Promises for Covenant Kids

CROSSWAY BOOKS BY SUSAN HUNT

By Design

My ABC Bible Verses

Spiritual Mothering

The True Woman

Heirs of the Covenant

Your Home—a Place of Grace

■

To Grandma Mac (Mary Kathryn McLaurin), the matriarch of our clan,
in honor of her eighty-fifth birthday

And to her great-grandchildren, the cousins:
Hunter, Mary Kate, Daniel, Susie, and Sam Barriault
Mac and Angus Hunt, Cassie and Scotty Coley

And in memory of Pop (Daniel L. McLaurin) and Annie Grace Barriault

The Cousins' Covenant
"They entered into a covenant to seek the LORD,
the God of their fathers, with all their heart and with all their soul."
2 Chronicles 15:12

Contents

Dear Parents:

This book is our effort to put the concepts from *Heirs of the Covenant* and *Your Home—A Place of Grace* into stories for children. We want children to have the glorious experience of discovering Jesus on every page of Scripture. We want them to see what the disciples saw.

We hear much today about family values. This is good, but it is not enough to turn up the volume on morality. The Bible is not simply a code of conduct. The Bible is God's revelation of Himself and His promise to send a Savior. God's covenant of grace is the thread woven all through Scripture. In this covenant God promises to be our God and to dwell among us. The covenant defines and unites us as God's people. A covenantal perspective of Scripture begins with the character of God, and the values of the covenant community reflect the character of God. We must help our children to learn more about who God is and what He has done for us and then pray that they will be transformed by this gospel message.

> *That very day two of them were going to a village named Emmaus, . . . and they were talking with each other about all these things that had happened. While they were talking and discussing together, Jesus himself drew near and went with them. But their eyes were kept from recognizing him. And he said to them, "What is this conversation that you are holding with each other as you walk?" And they stood still, looking sad. . . .*
>
> *And he said to them, "O foolish ones, and slow of heart to believe all that the prophets have spoken! Was it not necessary that the Christ should suffer these things and enter into his glory?" And beginning with Moses and all the Prophets, he interpreted to them in all the Scriptures the things concerning himself. . . .*
>
> *And their eyes were opened, and they recognized him. And he vanished from their sight. They said to each other, "Did not our hearts burn within us while he talked to us on the road, while he opened to us the Scriptures?" And they rose that same hour and returned to Jerusalem. And they found the eleven and those who were with them gathered together, saying, "The Lord has risen indeed. . . ." (Luke 24:13-17, 25-27, 31-34)*

When our children see Jesus in all of Scripture, then they will find others and proclaim, "It is true. . . . He is risen!"

You will see five basic principles woven into these stories:

FIRST, God made a covenant promise to redeem a people for Himself. He kept that promise by giving Jesus to fulfill the terms of the covenant.

SECOND, God is the reference point for all of life. These stories begin with the character of God as He shows us Himself in His Word and then identify a core value that reflects His character.

THIRD, God gives His children His Holy Spirit to empower us to trust and obey.

FOURTH, a covenantal approach to faith and life recognizes that when God adopts us as His children, we become part of His family. This glorious principle of covenant life is expressed through our connection to those in our local church.

FIFTH, a covenantal approach to faith and life is outward focused. We must always be eager to extend the boundaries of the covenant to reach others with the love and compassion of our Savior.

The first part of the book will lay the foundation. The second part will begin to explore some covenant values.

These family values will be countercultural because they do not exalt self; they glorify God. They reflect His goodness. These are the cultural values of the covenant community. . . .

There will be a commonality of core values for families who live in the realm of the covenant, because these are biblical ethics, but there will be different emphases, priorities, and expressions of these values among families and in different life seasons. This diversity is good. It will make the work and worship of God's family richer and healthier.

Each core value is an expression of the boldest initiative ever decreed: "'Love the Lord your God with all your heart and with all your soul and with all your mind.' This is the first and greatest commandment. And the second is like it: 'Love your neighbor as yourself'" (Matthew 22:37-39). (Taken from *Your Home—A Place of Grace*, p. 157)

For God's glory,
Susan and Richie

P.S. FROM SUSAN: God's gift of family leaves me breathless. As grandparents, Gene and I delight in helping our children and the young parents in our church show and tell their children the praiseworthy deeds of our God. As a mother, I rejoice in the privilege of working on this book with our son. My prayer is that the Lord will use this effort to equip young parents to "love the Lord your God with all your heart and with all your soul and with all your might . . . [and to] teach [His commandments] diligently to your children, and . . . talk of them when you sit in your house, and when you walk by the way, and when you lie down, and when you rise" (Deuteronomy 6:5-7).

P.S. FROM RICHIE: In my work as a director of children's ministry, I am very aware that my ministry is not just to the children. A covenantal approach to discipling children means that I see each child as part of a nuclear family and as part of the family of families—our local church. I pray that the Lord will use this book to extend that ministry beyond our covenant community to other families and churches. Our children are gifts to us as parents, but they are also treasures entrusted to our church family. My prayer is that we will be good stewards of these treasures.

HOW TO USE THIS BOOK

We have used these stories with children ages four to twelve. As younger children hear the stories, they will begin to learn the language and ways of covenant life. Older children will begin to comprehend a covenantal perspective of faith and life and will see how God's truth is integrated into all of life.

The questions at the end of each story will help you to evaluate your child's comprehension and application and will encourage additional conversations with him or her. Use the questions that match the maturity of your child. Each time you repeat the stories, you may want to use more questions.

We encourage you to memorize the Scripture verses with your children. Scripture memorization plants God's Word in their minds, and we can trust the Holy Spirit to use that Word to teach, convict, and convince them. If your children are younger, you may want to select just one or two verses to memorize.

Involve your children in the story. Let them answer questions and read the Bible verses.

When you as parents read through the stories in Part 2, talk about your situation, opportunities, and passions. Then prayerfully determine one core value that will begin to define your family. Ask the Lord to show you specific ways to activate this value in your family life. Once this value has become ingrained in the language and actions of your family, add another core value. Don't be limited by the particular values we have chosen to highlight. The possibilities are endless as we spend a lifetime of exploring "the love of Christ that surpasses knowledge, that you may be filled with all the fullness of God" (Ephesians 3:18-19).

PART 1

THE COVENANT WAY

CHAPTER ONE

The Mystery

CLUE #1:
Read Colossians 2:2-3 to discover where
the treasures of wisdom and knowledge are hidden.

My purpose is that they may be encouraged in heart and united in love, so that they may have the full riches of complete understanding, in order that they may know the mystery of God, namely, Christ, in whom are hidden all the treasures of wisdom and knowledge. (Colossians 2:2-3 NIV)

Late one afternoon Cassie, her brother Caleb, and their friend Daniel, who lived next door, sat on their front steps.

"Okay, let's make a plan for tomorrow," suggested Caleb. Caleb was the organized one.

"Well," said Cassie, "I feel like doing something important!"

"Ditto," replied Daniel. "We're having a great summer, but I think it's time we get down to serious business. I think we should do something really big—something that will get our pictures in the newspaper or on TV."

"Yeah," said Cassie as her eyes widened with excitement. "Maybe we can solve a mystery, find a treasure, or rescue a little kid."

Cassie and Daniel looked at Caleb.

"Why are you looking at me?" asked Caleb.

"Well, you're the one who said we need a plan. What do you think we should do?" asked Cassie.

"And make it something really important," chimed in Daniel.

Suddenly Caleb felt the weight of responsibility on his shoulders. His dad had been talking to him about being a leader, and now he needed to lead. "Well," he said slowly, "I think we need to give this careful thought."

The three friends sat on the steps in silence. The silence felt very uncomfortable to Caleb because he knew Cassie and Daniel expected him to come up with an idea. He was really beginning to squirm when he heard a familiar voice.

"Hello, lads and lassie. How are you today?"

Every day at this time, just like clockwork, Sir John passed their house. His real name was Mr. John Knox McDougal. Several months ago he had moved from Scotland to live with his daughter Miss Jenny. He always wore a plaid tie. He even played the bagpipe, and once he wore his Scottish kilt and played this extraordinary instrument in church. It was quite wonderful. The kids loved to listen to his Scottish accent, and somehow they knew that he loved to listen to them. The children were not sure why everyone called him Sir John, but it was a perfect fit for this polite gentleman.

"We're doing great, Sir John," said Cassie in her grown-up voice. Caleb rolled his eyes, the way big brothers do sometimes. "We're making our plans for tomorrow, and we're going to do something very important."

"Yeah," said Daniel. "Like solve a mystery or rescue a little kid. We may even be on TV. We're just waiting for Caleb to come up with an idea."

"Ummm," said Sir John. "That sounds exciting. Any ideas yet, Caleb?"

"Well, I'm thinking," said Caleb slowly.

Sir John seemed to understand Caleb's difficulty. "Why don't you come walk with me, lad," he suggested. "We can have a man-to-man talk."

Caleb sighed with relief. Help had arrived just in the nick of time.

As the two walked, Sir John said, "Caleb, would you three really like to do something important this summer?"

"Sure," said Caleb. "But I don't know

any mystery that needs to be solved. And even if there was a kid who needed to be rescued, I'm sure they'd call 911 instead of us."

"Caleb, my boy, I'm talking about something even more important than those things," declared Sir John.

"Really?" asked Caleb amazed. "What is it?"

"Well, this is my plan . . ."

Cassie and Daniel sat patiently on the front steps. Finally they saw Caleb and Sir John turn the corner. Sir John went into his house, and Caleb ran all the way home.

"This is *so* . . . good," Caleb panted as he ran into the yard. "We . . . are going to . . . solve a mystery . . . and find . . . *rich treasures!*"

Cassie was speechless, but Daniel said, "Now this sounds really good. Tell us more."

Caleb's breathing was slowing down, so he explained, "This is going to be a great adventure that will last all summer. Sir John told me about a verse in the Bible that says that knowing more about Jesus is like solving the mystery of who God is. He said that we will discover treasures of wisdom and knowledge. Every week Sir John is going to tell us something that the Bible teaches about God. Then we'll learn about something we're supposed to be and do because of what we learn about God. Sir John calls it covenant values. It's all about how we live as God's covenant family."

Cassie and Daniel tried not to look disappointed, but finally Cassie said, "Well, it's not exactly what I had in mind."

"I don't think it will get us on TV," complained Daniel.

"How is that an adventure?" asked Cassie.

"Well," explained Caleb, "Sir John is going to give us notebooks with clues, and we'll use the clues to find the covenant values. Trust me, it's going to be really good. We start first thing tomorrow morning at Sir John's house—9:30 sharp."

Cassie, Caleb, and Daniel are about to embark on an unforgettable journey where they will discover treasures of wisdom and knowledge. I do hope you will join them.

———■———

LET'S TALK

What did Cassie, Caleb, and Daniel want to do?

Who offered to help them?

What is the mystery he is going to help them solve?

What are the treasures they will discover?

Let's memorize God's Word: Colossians 2:2-3

———■———

LET'S PRAY

Pray that you will understand more of the mystery of God and that you will discover His treasures of wisdom and knowledge.

CHAPTER TWO

Sir John's House

CLUE #1:
Look up Colossians 2:2-3 to discover where the treasures of wisdom and knowledge are hidden.

My purpose is that they may be encouraged in heart and united in love, so that they may have the full riches of complete understanding, in order that they may know the mystery of God, namely, Christ, in whom are hidden all the treasures of wisdom and knowledge. (Colossians 2:2-3 NIV)

———■———

"You know, Caleb," admitted Cassie as they walked to Sir John's house, "when you told us about our summer adventure, I didn't think it sounded very exciting. But I was wrong. Just going to Sir John's house is an adventure."

"Yeah," said Daniel. "This should be fun."

When they rang the doorbell, Miss Jenny opened the door and held out her arms to hug the children. "Oh, I'm so happy to see you!" she exclaimed. "Dear Papa has been preparing for your arrival." She led them into Sir John's library.

"Hello, lads and lassie," Sir John greeted them warmly. "Please sit down."

As the children settled on the huge sofa in front of Sir John's desk, they noticed the soft sound of bagpipe music. The room smelled of old books and leather, the fragrance of fresh flowers from Miss Jenny's garden, and best of all the delicious whiff of cookies baking in the kitchen. Sir John was wearing a plaid vest. He looked quite sharp.

"That's a cool vest," Caleb remarked. "It's just like the ties you wear."

"That it is, my lad." Sir John smiled. "This is my clan tartan. In Scotland every clan has a special plaid that shows that we belong to that family. But now it's time for us to begin our adventure, and then we'll have some of Miss Jenny's shortbread cookies and milk. There's nothing better than warm Scottish short-bread. Ah Scotland! Would you like for me to tell you a story about a fearless Scottish woman named Jenny Geddes? My dear daughter is named for this woman."

The children felt as if they were entering into a world of memories.

Sir John's eyes sparkled as he began. "Many, many years ago—even before America was discovered but several years after the great preacher John Knox made his mark on Scotland—by the way, children, I was named for this great preacher." (The children were soon to learn that Sir John loved to find any reason to mention his hero.)

"Well," continued Sir John, "it was a dark and troubled time in Scotland's history. Scotland's king was sinful, and his heart was hardened against God. He said that he had authority over God's church, but God's people knew this was not right. John Knox had taught them well, and they knew that Jesus is the sovereign King of the church."

Sir John paused so the children could think about this, and then he proceeded with the story. "Jenny Geddes was just an ordinary fruit-seller. She was not an educated woman, but she knew God's Word. In those days there were no pews or chairs in the churches. The people stood, or they brought their own lit-tle stools. One Sunday the king sent a preacher to speak in the church in Edinburgh. The preacher began to say things that were not true to God's Word. This was a dangerous situation for the people. Would they be silent when God was not honored? This preacher was one of the king's men. He could have all of them put in prison. Everyone was frozen with fear—except Jenny Geddes. Feisty Jenny picked up her stool and threw it at the pulpit."

Cassie was shocked. "She threw it at the pulpit?"

Sir John smiled. "I know that seems unbelievable, but you must remember that these were difficult days. Jenny Geddes's courage gave others courage, and they picked up whatever they could find and started throwing it. Soon God's people all over Scotland were encouraged to be faithful to God's Word. Hundreds of them signed an agreement insisting that Jesus is King of His church. This agreement was called a 'covenant,' and those who signed it became known as the 'covenanters.' Their motto was 'For Christ's Crown and Covenant.' Many men and women, and even boys and girls, suffered and died because of their faithfulness to Christ's crown and this covenant."

Suddenly Cassie remembered something she had noticed when they walked into Sir John's library. She turned and looked at the wall behind her. "Sir John," she asked excitedly, "is that why you have that beautiful banner hanging on your wall?" The other children turned and saw the banner with the words "For Christ's Crown and Covenant" written on it.

Sir John smiled. "Ah, lassie, I was hoping one of you would notice." He handed each of them a notebook with a banner on the cover just like the one on his wall. "Now the detective work begins," he announced. He told the children to open their journals, and he asked Caleb to read the first clue. Caleb read, "'Look up Colossians 2:2-3 to discover where the treasures of wisdom and knowledge are hidden.'"

All three children started turning pages in their Bibles. "I've got it!" said Daniel, and he read: "'My purpose is that they may be encouraged in heart and united in love, so that they may have the full riches of complete understanding, in order that they may know the mystery of God, namely, Christ, in whom are hidden all the treasures of wisdom and knowledge.'"

"So the treasures of wisdom and knowledge are hidden in Jesus," said Caleb.

"Right you are, my young scholar," replied Sir John. "When Jesus came to earth, He showed what God is like. Jesus revealed the mystery of who God is. The Bible tells us about Jesus, and so when we read it, we should always be trying to discover some of the treasures of wisdom and knowledge that are hidden in Him."

Cassie closed her journal and looked at the banner on its cover. "I think I understand about the crown. Kings wear crowns, and Jesus is the King. But what is His covenant?"

"Well, Lassie, that is your next clue," answered Sir John. "Before you come back next week, I want you to do three things. First, look up all of the verses listed under Clue #2 to discover the answer to your question. Second, memorize the verse I have checked. Now please turn to the next page in your journals."

"But there's nothing on this page except the days of the week," said Daniel.

"Why, you are the smart one," laughed Sir John. "This is the third thing I want you to do. Every day write 'For Christ's Crown and Covenant.' As you write it, remember that many covenanters suffered and died because they said that Jesus was their sovereign King. Ask the Lord to help you to *live* for King Jesus. Pray that you will be fearless in following Him. And I will be praying that as you read and memorize the Bible verses, you will discover some of the treasures of wisdom and knowledge that are hidden in Christ. Now I think it's time for shortbread and milk."

———■———

LET'S TALK

Who was Sir John named for?

Who was Miss Jenny named for?

What did Jenny Geddes do when the preacher preached things that were not true to God's Word?

What was the covenanters' motto?

Where are the treasures of wisdom and knowledge hidden?

Let's memorize God's Word: Colossians 2:2-3

———■———

LET'S PRAY

Pray that you will discover some of the treasures of wisdom and knowledge that are hidden in Jesus.

CHAPTER THREE

The Covenant Promise

CLUE #2:
Read these verses to discover the covenant promise.

I will establish my covenant between me and you and your offspring after you throughout their generations for an everlasting covenant, to be God to you and to your offspring after you. (Genesis 17:7)

I will take you to be my people, and I will be your God, and you shall know that I am the Lord your God, who has brought you out from under the burdens of the Egyptians. (Exodus 6:7)

I will make my dwelling among you, and my soul shall not abhor you. I will walk among you and will be your God, and you shall be my people.

(Leviticus 26:11-12)

But this is the covenant that I will make with the house of Israel after those days, declares the Lord: I will put my law within them, and I will write it on their hearts. And I will be their God, and they shall be my people.

(Jeremiah 31:33 and Hebrews 8:10)

I will bring them to dwell in the midst of Jerusalem. And they shall be my people, and I will be their God, in faithfulness and in righteousness. (Zechariah 8:8)

. . . God said, "I will make my dwelling among them and walk among them, and I will be their God, and they shall be my people." (2 Corinthians 6:16)

Then I saw a new heaven and a new earth, for the first heaven and the first earth had passed away, and the sea was no more. And I saw the holy city, new Jerusalem, coming down out of heaven from God, prepared as a bride adorned for her husband. And I heard a loud voice from the throne saying, "Behold, the dwelling place of God is with man. He will dwell with them, and they will be his people, and God himself will be with them as their God." (Revelation 21:1-3)

"Well, Caleb," said Daniel as they walked home from Sir John's, "that was more fun than I expected. I think this is going to be a great adventure."

"I loved it!" exclaimed Cassie. "Sir John tells such neat stories, and Miss Jenny is so sweet, and our journals are so wonderful, and I had such a good time, and—"

"Okay, Cassie," Caleb interrupted, "we get the picture."

Cassie became quite chatty when she was excited, and she was excited now. She could hardly wait to show her mom the journal Sir John gave her. As soon as she walked into their house, she started talking again. The boys ran out to play, but Cassie told her mother every detail of their visit to Sir John's. When they looked at the clues in her journal, her mom said, "Cassie, I have a great idea for our family devotions tonight. Come with me. This will be so good."

That night during the family devotional time, Cassie and Caleb showed their journals to their dad. "We're supposed to work on Clue #2 for next week," said Cassie, "and Mom and I are ready." Then she read the clue: "'Look up these verses to discover the covenant promise.'"

"Cassie and I wrote all of the verses they are supposed to look up on these cards," their mom explained. "And we attached them to this red ribbon. Let's each take two of the cards and read them. See if you can find the promise made in each verse."

They all sat in a circle holding the red ribbon. Each of them read two of the verses.

"I see it!" cried Caleb. "In every verse God promises that He will be our God."

"And He says that we will be His people," added Cassie.

"What wise covenant kids we have," teased their dad. "Now look closely and see if you see something else repeated several times."

"I think I see it," ventured Caleb. "God says He will live among us."

"Exactly!" said his dad. "God promises that He will be our God, we will be His people, and He will live among us. Now look at the verses again. Where is the covenant promise found in the Bible? Is it at the beginning, at the end, or where?"

Cassie and Caleb flipped through the cards, and at the same time they said, "It's everywhere!"

"Yes!" exclaimed their dad. "All through the Bible God promises that He will be our God, we will be His people, and He will live among us."

"Now I have a question," said their mom. "Why do you think we put these verses on a red ribbon?"

"I think it's because we are saved by the blood of Jesus," Cassie replied.

"Yes, Cassie." Her mom smiled. "God kept His covenant promise when Jesus came and lived among us on this earth. He died for our sins so that we can be God's people."

"I think your journals are great," said their dad. "Let me see the other clues."

Cassie sat on her dad's lap as he looked at her journal. "Well, this is really interesting," he commented. He read Clue #1: "'Look up Colossians 2:2-3 to discover where the treasures of wisdom and knowledge are hidden.'" Dad opened his Bible and read: "'My purpose is that they may be encouraged in heart and united in love, so that they may have the full riches of complete understanding, in order that they may know the mystery of God, namely, Christ, in whom are hidden all the treasures of wisdom and knowledge.'"

Dad looked at the children. "You know, Cassie and Caleb, every time the elders in our church meet, we pray this Scripture for our church family. We want our congregation to be encouraged in heart and united in love so we will all know Jesus better and better. In fact, your mom and I want to tell you about someone in our church family who needs to be encouraged, and we have an idea about how to encourage her."

"Who?" asked Cassie and Caleb together.

"It's Granny Grace," answered Mom.

Mrs. Stevens was a widow who lived across the street from Cassie and Caleb's family. All the children at church and in the neighborhood called her Granny Grace. She had taught the Sunday school class for five-year-olds since Cassie and Caleb's mom was a little girl.

"You see," continued their dad, "Granny Grace's daughter and grandchildren are coming to visit her for a while, and they aren't Christians. We need to pray for them, and we need to show them God's love. Your mom and I thought we would have a party to welcome them."

"Let's have a cookout," suggested Cassie.

"That's exactly what we had in mind," laughed their mom.

"I have a great idea," said Caleb. "Let's invite Sir John and Miss Jenny and Daniel and his mom and dad and Pastor Scotty and his family. Then Angus will be here."

Cassie added, "And Susie!"

Angus and Susie were Pastor Scotty's children, and the same ages as Cassie and Caleb.

"That's exactly what we had in mind," laughed their dad.

On Friday night everyone came with bowls and trays of food. Granny Grace brought her famous banana pudding, and of course Miss Jenny brought a huge tray of shortbread. They all gathered in the backyard, and Granny Grace introduced her daughter and the grandchildren, Mary and Mac. The children played while the adults cooked hamburgers and got everything ready. All the kids tried to make Mary and Mac feel welcome. When the food was ready, everyone joined hands in a big circle, and Pastor Scotty thanked God for good food and good fellowship.

After dinner Caleb looked at Sir John and asked, "Well, did you bring it?"

"I did," grinned Sir John.

Caleb stood up on a bench and announced, "Ladies and gentlemen, may I have your attention? It is my great pleasure to present, all the way from Scotland, Sir John—the world's finest bagpipe player."

Well, I don't know if you have ever heard a bagpipe or not, but it is a really loud instrument. Everyone laughed and clapped as Sir John played. Then he played "Amazing Grace," and everyone sang. It was wonderful.

When it was time to leave, Granny Grace hugged Cassie and Caleb and whispered, "Thank you for being so kind to Mary and Mac. You encouraged me tonight. I'm so thankful for my covenant family. Jesus promised that when we gather together in His name, He is with us, and I felt His presence tonight."

Cassie's eyes opened wide. "There's the covenant promise again!" she declared. "God promised to be our God and to live among us."

"Indeed," agreed Granny Grace. "And His presence among us is what encourages our hearts and unites us in love."

LET'S TALK

What is the covenant promise?

Where is this promise found in the Bible?

*Why did Cassie and her mom attach the
Bible verses to a red ribbon?*

What did their family do to encourage Granny Grace?

*Granny Grace told Cassie and Caleb that
Jesus promised something. What was it?*

Look up Matthew 18:20 in your Bible to find this promise.

Let's memorize God's Word: 2 Corinthians 6:16.

LET'S PRAY

Thank God that He is your God and that you are His child.
Thank Him for your church family and pray that they
will be encouraged in heart and united in love.

IDEA FOR PARENTS: *Like the family in the story, you may want to write these verses on cards
and attach them to a red ribbon.*

CHAPTER FOUR

For Christ's Crown and Covenant

CLUE #3:
Read Jeremiah 24:7 to discover how God makes us willing and able to believe the covenant promise and to live for Christ's crown and covenant.

I will give them a heart to know that I am the LORD, and they shall be my people and I will be their God. . . . (Jeremiah 24:7)

Cassie, Caleb, and Daniel rang the doorbell. Miss Jenny welcomed them. "Oh, children, I found some pictures that I want to show you," she said as she led them to Sir John's library.

"Ummm," said Daniel, "I think I smell yummy Scottish shortbread."

"That you do, lad," said Sir John as he stood to greet them. "Miss Jenny always has shortbread for our guests. And today she has pictures for you to see. Do you remember the story I told you last week?"

"Sure," replied Cassie. "It was about feisty Jenny Geddes. She threw her stool at the preacher because he was not preaching that Jesus is the King of the church."

"And about the covenanters whose motto was 'For Christ's Crown and Covenant,'" added Caleb.

Miss Jenny held out a photo album. "Miss Jenny, that's you," said Cassie, pointing to a photo. "What is that you're standing beside? It looks like a stool on top of a post."

"Yes, it does," laughed Miss Jenny. "This is a monument that women in Scotland had set up in memory of Jenny Geddes. It's in the church in Edinburgh."

"Wow," said Daniel. "I guess that makes you famous."

"Oh no, child," laughed Miss Jenny. "It just makes me very happy that I'm named for a woman who was not afraid to stand firm for King Jesus. And it makes me want to be fearless in obeying Him."

Cassie noticed that Sir John was a bit tearful. She decided that parents never get too old to want their covenant children to know the treasures of wisdom and knowledge that are hidden in Jesus.

"Now look at this picture," instructed Miss Jenny.

"It's Sir John," observed Daniel. "He's standing beside a statue. Let me guess . . . is this a statue of John Knox? Knox looks pretty feisty too."

They all laughed, and Sir John said, "Ah yes, my boy. Fearless he was. It was once written that he was 'one who never feared the face of man.' John Knox said that he was not his own master, but he was bound to obey Jesus."

Sir John looked at the children. "Perhaps, just perhaps, one of you will be the next John Knox." And then he looked at Cassie and grinned. "Or Jenny Geddes. And now, my young scholars, let us begin. Tell me what treasures you discovered this week."

The children opened their journals.

"We memorized the covenant promise," Cassie told him.

"Splendid," beamed Sir John. "What is the covenant promise?"

It was like music to the old gentleman's ears to hear the children say, "'. . . God said, *I will make my dwelling among them and walk among them, and I will be their God, and they shall be my people*' (2 Corinthians 6:16)."

"Ah, what a glorious promise," declared Sir John. "And now did you write 'For Christ's Crown and Covenant' in your journals each day?"

"You tell him, Daniel," urged Cassie.

"Well, we wrote it every day, but we also decided to say it to each other when we met outside to play. After a couple of days, it just sort of took over our minds. We were thinking about it all the time. And then the coolest thing happened. You remember Mary and Mac—Granny Grace's grandchildren?"

Sir John nodded.

"Well," explained Daniel, "Granny Grace asked us to pray for them because they're not Christians."

"We've prayed, and we've really been trying to be nice to them," added Cassie.

Daniel continued, "We were all playing in the backyard when they wanted to go inside and watch TV. They said it was time for their favorite program."

"That's when it all started," said Cassie. "The program they wanted to watch was one our parents don't let us see. I didn't know what to do."

Daniel said, "I guess we were all a little shy, but fearless Caleb came to the rescue."

"What did you do, Caleb?" asked Sir John.

"Well," said Caleb, "I kept thinking about 'For Christ's Crown and Covenant.' It was rolling over and over in my head."

Cassie replied, "Caleb was real nice, but he told them that our parents don't allow us to watch that program because it will turn our hearts to worthless things. You see, Sir John," she explained, "every morning at breakfast our family prays this verse from the Bible: 'Turn my heart toward your statutes and not toward selfish gain. Turn my eyes away from worthless things; preserve my life according to your word' (Psalm 119:36-37 NIV)."

"Splendid, splendid!" exclaimed Sir John. "Because of Christ's crown and covenant you children obeyed your parents, and you stood firm for what is good and right. But what did Mary and Mac say?"

"Well," said Caleb, "they shrugged and went home, but I don't think Granny Grace let them watch the program because in just a few minutes we saw them come back outside, and they didn't seem too happy."

"Sir John," asked Cassie, "we were wondering if we could invite Mary and Mac to come here with us. Would it be okay?"

"Ah, children, you've made my old heart quite joyful. Of course you may invite them. But we must pray that they will want to join us and that they will want to know God—which reminds me of the clue I have for you today."

The children looked in their journals and saw Clue #3: "'Look up Jeremiah 24:7 to discover how God makes us willing and able to believe the covenant promise and to live for Christ's crown and covenant.'" They all picked up their Bibles and started turning the pages.

"I found it," called Daniel. He read: "'I will give them a heart to know that I am the LORD, and they shall be my people and I will be their God. . . .'"

"There's the covenant promise," Caleb pointed out.

"Yes, but look closer. Do your detective work," instructed Sir John. "Pretend you have spiritual spyglasses and you are inspecting the evidence to discover what has to happen before we are willing and able to believe the covenant promise."

The children pretended to look at the verse through a magnifying glass. Suddenly Daniel shouted, "I see it. God gives us a heart to know Him!"

"Good work, Detective Dan," Sir John praised him. "You see, our hearts are so sinful that we will not want to know God or to live for Christ's crown and covenant until God gives us new hearts. Well, my young friends, you are solving the mystery and discovering treasures of wisdom and knowledge. And now I think it's time for refreshments."

LET'S TALK

What was the covenanters' motto?

When the children were playing, what did Mary and Mac want to do?

Why was this a problem?

What did Caleb remember?

What did he say to Mary and Mac?

How does God make us willing and able to believe the covenant promise and to live for Christ's crown and covenant?

Let's memorize God's Word: Jeremiah 24:7.

LET'S PRAY

Thank the Lord that He gives us a heart that can know Him. Thank Him that He is our God and we are His people.

CHAPTER FIVE

The Plan

CLUE #3:
Read Jeremiah 24:7 to discover how God
makes us willing and able to believe the covenant
promise and to live for Christ's crown and covenant.

I will give them a heart to know that I am the LORD, and they shall be my people and I will be their God. . . . (Jeremiah 24:7)

———■———

"Hello, children," Sir John greeted Cassie, Caleb, and Daniel as they walked into his library.

The three settled onto the leather couch. They looked rather gloomy.

"Well," began Caleb, "we tried. We asked Mary and Mac to come with us, but they rolled their eyes and laughed. They think they're too cool to come, Sir John."

"And they think we're really weird," added Daniel.

"I think we need a plan to get them to want to come," said Caleb, the organized one.

"Just a minute, lad," said Sir John. "Don't you remember our clue from last week? What has to happen before we are willing and able to believe the covenant promise?"

Cassie, Caleb, and Daniel perked up as they said with great enthusiasm: "'I will give them a heart to know that I am the LORD, and they shall be my people and I will be their God. . . .' (Jeremiah 24:7)."

"But how does that help us to have a plan to get Mary and Mac to come with us?" asked Cassie.

Sir John smiled. "You see, lassie, none of your plans can make Mary and Mac want to know about Jesus. But what you can do is to pray that God will give them a heart to know Him. And you can show them God's grace and mercy by being loving and kind to them."

Always one to say what she felt or thought, Cassie spoke up. "You don't understand, Sir John. It's just no fun being with them. They really do have an attitude problem. They make us feel like we're silly. I guess we're sort of afraid of them."

"Ahhh," said Sir John. "Yes, I do understand. But not to bother. I have a splendid story for you today."

Miss Jenny walked into the room, and the children stood to greet her. "Hello, Miss Jenny," grinned Daniel, the charmer. "Is that your delicious shortbread I smell?"

Miss Jenny laughed and assured the children that the shortbread would be ready soon.

"Now, my fine scholars," said Sir John, "let me tell you a story. Have I told you about John Knox?" Sir John had a mischievous grin on his face. He knew that he always told them about John Knox.

"Yes, sir!" Daniel replied politely. "He was the great, fearless preacher of Scotland, and you are named for him."

Sir John smiled. "Right you are, lad. Why, Mary the Queen was more afraid of the prayers of John Knox than of all the armies of Europe. John Knox's daughter Elizabeth was also quite fearless. She married John Welch, another great preacher of God's Word. One day he was arrested and put in prison for preaching God's truth. It made Elizabeth sad for her dear husband to be in such a dreadful place. She missed him and needed him at home. It was hard trying to take care of the family alone. Elizabeth asked many times to see the king to beg him to let her husband go. Finally she was told that the king would see her."

"Wow," said Cassie, "she must have been scared."

"Well, lassie," said Sir John, "remember that Elizabeth's father was a preacher who never feared the face of man. I suppose Elizabeth trusted God just as her father had done."

It was obvious that Cassie loved this story. "Elizabeth sure was brave to go see the same king who put her husband in jail."

Sir John nodded.

"I like Elizabeth," said Cassie, the chatty one.

"So what happened, Sir John?" asked Daniel.

"Did the king throw her in prison?" asked Caleb.

The boys were getting a bit impatient with Cassie. They wanted to hear the rest of the story.

Sir John continued, "When Elizabeth stood before the king's throne, he looked at her and smirked. 'Well,

Mrs. Welch, if you will persuade your husband to say that I am king of the land and king of the church, I will let him go.'"

"Oh no!" cried Cassie. "Poor Elizabeth. What did she do, Sir John?"

"Elizabeth's heart was racing. She longed for her beloved husband to come home. She knew that the king could have her husband's head cut off, but she was fearless in her obedience to King Jesus. Elizabeth stood straight and looked the king right in the eye. She lifted her apron and said, 'I would rather have his head in this,' and she turned and walked out."

"Yeaaa, Elizabeth!" shouted Cassie. "She was as fearless as her daddy."

"Yes, Cassie, she was," said Sir John. "This dear woman loved her husband, but she knew that Jesus is the King of His church. She preferred to do without her husband than to have him deny King Jesus."

Cassie, the chatty one, moaned, "Yikes! I guess that nails us. Elizabeth was not afraid for her husband to remain in prison, but we're afraid to be friends with Mary and Mac."

Caleb, the organized one, said, "I still think we need a plan—but it needs to be a plan to pray that God will give Mary and Mac a heart to want to know Him."

Daniel, the charmer, said, "And we need a plan to be loving and kind to them."

Miss Jenny, the hospitable one, said, "And now, children, come to my kitchen for shortbread and milk."

———■———

LET'S TALK

Why were Cassie, Caleb, and Daniel sad?

What did Caleb think they needed?

How did Sir John say they needed to pray?

What did he say they needed to do?

What did you learn about John Knox's daughter?

What kind of plan did the children decide they needed?

Let's memorize God's Word: Jeremiah 24:7.

LET'S PRAY

Do you know someone who does not know and love the Lord Jesus?
Pray that God will give that person a heart to know Him.

MISS JENNY'S SHORTBREAD

1 lb. butter or margarine
1 cup sugar
4 cups all-purpose flour
2 teaspoons almond flavoring

Soften butter and mix all ingredients with a mixer.
Form dough into a roll and wrap it in waxed paper.
Chill the roll in the refrigerator. Slice the dough into
cookies and bake at 350° for 20 to 30 minutes—
until light brown on the bottom. Do not overbake.

CHAPTER SIX

The Circus

CLUE #4:

Are we God's covenant people because we are better or smarter than other people? Look up Deuteronomy 7:6-8 to discover why we are God's covenant people.

For you are a people holy to the LORD your God. The LORD your God has chosen you to be a people for his treasured possession, out of all the peoples who are on the face of the earth. It was not because you were more in number than any other people that the LORD set his love on you and chose you . . . but it is because the LORD loves you. . . . (Deuteronomy 7:6-8)

"We've tried. We have really tried," moaned Cassie as her family gathered for family worship. "We've prayed for Mary and Mac, and we've tried to be nice to them. But it's no use. They are just plain mean."

"I could take the name-calling and acting like we're weird, but when Mary tripped Cassie today and then just laughed and ran off—well, that did it. If she had been a boy, I would have tackled her," proclaimed Caleb.

"I guess they're just too bad to become Christians," decided Cassie.

"Well, kids," said their dad, "I can understand why you're so frustrated. They *have* been pretty brutal with you. But are they really too bad to become Christians? Do we believe in Jesus because we're good? Get your journals and look at Clue #4."

Caleb opened his journal and read: "'Are we God's covenant people because we are better or smarter than other people? Look up Deuteronomy 7:6-8 to discover why we are God's covenant people.'"

They all opened their Bibles, and their dad read: "'For you are a people holy to the LORD your God.

The LORD your God has chosen you to be a people for his treasured possession, out of all the peoples who are on the face of the earth. It was not because you were more in number than any other people that the LORD set his love on you and chose you . . . but it is because the LORD loves you. . . .'"

"Umm," said Caleb. "I guess I'm God's child because He chose me."

"Right!" said his dad. "And why did He choose you? Is it because you are so great or powerful or good?"

"I see it," offered Cassie. "It's because He loves us."

"Right again," said their dad. "None of us is good enough to be God's child. The only reason you love the Lord Jesus is because God first loved you and set His love on you. We need to keep praying that God will give Mary and Mac new hearts so they can know Him."

"Kids," said their mother, "your dad and I have decided that you need to know a little more about Mary and Mac. Maybe that will help you to keep being kind to them, and it will help you to understand how much we need to pray for them."

Cassie and Caleb noticed tears in their mother's eyes as she continued. "You see, Mary and Mac are not just visiting Granny Grace. They had to move here because their dad left their mom, and she had to get a job to support them."

"Oh no!" sighed Cassie. "Poor Mary."

"That's terrible," said Caleb. "I'll bet they're really sad."

"Let's think about how you would feel," said their dad.

"I think I'd be afraid," Cassie admitted.

"I think I'd be mad at the whole world," added Caleb.

"I think you're both exactly right," said their mom. "They're probably really frightened and angry, and they're taking it out on you kids."

"What can we do?" asked Cassie.

"Well," said their dad, "we can keep praying for them, and we can ask the Lord to give you wisdom and grace to show them God's love. It won't be easy, but as you do this, a wonderful thing will happen."

"What?" asked Cassie and Caleb at the same time.

Their dad smiled. "You will discover some of the treasures of wisdom and knowledge that are hidden in Christ. As you obey God's Word, even when it's hard, you get to know Him better. And knowing Him is the best treasure in all the world."

The next day the greatest thing happened. Well, first a terrible thing happened . . . then the great thing happened. The terrible thing was that Cassie and Caleb were playing with their remote control cars on the sidewalk, and Mac whizzed by on his bicycle and ran over Caleb's car. "Sorry," he said sarcastically as he sped off.

Cassie was trying to comfort Caleb when their dad drove up. "Hey, kids," he said. "Great news. Someone gave me six front-row tickets to the big circus that's coming to town this weekend. Each of you can invite a friend to go with us."

"Yeaaaa!" they both yelled. They forgot about the crushed toy.

"Who do you want to invite?" asked their dad.

"Daniel, of course," replied Caleb just as Daniel ran across his yard.

"What?" asked Daniel. Cassie and Caleb laughed.

"Dad has six tickets to the circus, and I'm inviting you," Caleb announced.

Daniel clapped his hands excitedly.

"How about you, Cassie?" asked her dad. "Are you going to ask Susie?"

Cassie looked very thoughtful. "No, I think I'll invite Mary."

"Why would you ask her?" questioned Daniel.

"Because I want to show her God's love," said Cassie. Then she told him about Mary and Mac's dad.

Everyone was quiet for a few moments, and then Daniel said, "Cassie, it's really cool that you want to take Mary." He looked at Caleb and said, "Thanks for inviting me, Caleb, but I think you should take Mac."

Cassie was the first to speak. "Daniel, that's really, really cool."

"I think we'd better go invite them before we change our minds," suggested Caleb.

When they knocked, Granny Grace came to the door. "Hello, kids," she said.

"Hi, Granny Grace," Caleb greeted her. "We came to ask Mary and Mac to go to the circus with us Saturday. Someone gave Dad some tickets."

Suddenly Mary and Mac were at the door. "You want to take us to the circus?" Mac gasped.

"Why would you want to take us?" asked Mary.

"We want to be your friends," replied Cassie.

"But I've been so mean to you," Mary reminded her.

"And I broke your remote control car," Mac said to Caleb.

No one said anything. After a few moments Granny Grace spoke up. "I think I understand. Mary and Mac, I've been telling you about the Lord Jesus, and I've been praying that you will know about His love. He has sent Cassie and Caleb to show you His love."

And so it happened that Mary, Mac, Cassie, and Caleb had a wonderful time at the circus. It was even more fun because Daniel's mom and dad got tickets, and they went to the circus too.

LET'S TALK

Why did Cassie think that Mary and Mac would not become Christians?

Is anyone too bad to become a Christian?

Do we believe in Jesus because we're good?

Why did God set His love on us?

What terrible thing happened in the story?

What was the great thing that happened?

Why did Cassie want to invite Mary to the circus?

What did Daniel do?

Let's memorize God's Word: Deuteronomy 7:6-8.

■

LET'S PRAY

Thank God that He has chosen you to be His treasured possession.
Thank Him that He loves you so much.

CHAPTER SEVEN

Cassie Discovers a Treasure

CLUE #5:
Read Matthew 1:23 to discover how God
would keep the covenant promise.

"Behold, the virgin shall conceive and bear a son, and they shall call his name Immanuel" (which means, God with us). (Matthew 1:23)

Clue #6:
Read John 3:16 to discover why God
would make such a wonderful promise.

For God so loved the world, that he gave his only Son, that whoever believes in him should not perish but have eternal life. (John 3:16)

——————■——————

Cassie was sitting in the big chair on her front porch. She loved being outside. She could think better when she could hear the birds and feel the fresh air. Sometimes when the sun was shining on her, she would get so cozy and comfortable that she would take a little snooze.

Suddenly she remembered that the next day they would go to Sir John's house, and they were supposed to find the answers to two clues. "Oops," she said. "I'd better get busy." She ran inside to get her journal and her Bible.

When she came back outside, she was surprised to see Mary standing on her porch.

"Hi, Mary," said Cassie in her friendliest voice.

Mary would not look at Cassie but instead stared down at her shoes. She was very uncomfortable. "Hi," she mumbled. "I had a good time at the circus. Thanks for taking me."

Cassie looked straight at Mary and smiled. "Thank you for going with me." Cassie knew that good manners are one way to show God's love to other people because gracious manners make others feel welcome and comfortable.

Mary seemed to relax. "What are you doing?" she asked.

"I'm working on my journal. Would you like to see it?" asked Cassie. "Come, sit down, and I'll show it to you. We are on an adventure," she explained. "We're trying to solve a mystery and discover treasures."

"A mystery . . . treasures . . . wow! What kind of treasures?" asked Mary as both girls settled into one of the chairs, and Cassie put her Bible on the table.

Cassie prayed silently, *Lord, please make me fearless now.* "Treasures of wisdom and knowledge that are hidden in Jesus," she replied and then held her breath. Would Mary laugh at her or call her a name?

Mary's face looked like one big question mark. "What are you talking about?" she asked.

Cassie realized that Mary was not being mean or sarcastic, that she really wanted to know. So Cassie quickly prayed in her heart, *Dear Jesus, give me wisdom and knowledge to know what to say.*

"You see, Mary," Cassie explained, "every week when we go to Sir John's house, he gives us clues with a Bible verse. The verses teach us things about Jesus, and knowing Jesus is like having great treasures of wisdom and knowledge."

"I have no idea what you're talking about," admitted Mary.

"Here, look at my journal," offered Cassie as she showed Mary all the clues and the answers she had written down. "I'm supposed to find the answers to Clues #5 and #6 for tomorrow. Would you like to help me?"

"Sure," answered Mary.

Cassie read Clue #5: "'Look up Matthew 1:23 to discover how God would keep the covenant promise.'"

Then she opened her Bible and read: "'Behold, the virgin shall conceive and bear a son, and they shall call his name Immanuel (which means, God with us)' (Matthew 1:23)."

"Oh! I think I get it!" squealed Cassie. "Look, Mary." Cassie quickly turned back to Clue #2 and pointed to the covenant promise. "God promised that He will be our God, we will be His people, and He will live among us."

"I don't understand," admitted Mary.

"Don't you see?" said Cassie excitedly. "This verse is talking about Jesus. One of His names is Immanuel—which means, 'God with us.' Jesus left heaven and came to live on this earth. He lived *among us* so He could die for our sins."

"Now I'm really confused. Why would He die for us? And isn't heaven supposed to be a happy place?" asked Mary.

"Oh yes," replied Cassie. "Heaven is perfect. There's no sin and no sadness in heaven."

Mary shook her head. "Then why would Jesus leave a perfectly happy place to come here where there is so much sadness?"

Cassie was just a little girl, but God had given her a very sensitive heart. Suddenly she remembered how sad Mary must feel because her daddy had left their family. Feeling Mary's sadness, Cassie prayed silently, *Dear Jesus, please show me how to comfort Mary.* She looked down and saw the next clue. She knew this was the answer to her prayer.

"Look, Mary, the next clue will answer your question." She read Clue #6: "'Look up John 3:16 to discover why God would make such a wonderful promise.'" Cassie had memorized this verse, and so she said it without even turning to it in her Bible. "'For God so loved the world, that he gave his only Son, that whoever believes in him should not perish but have eternal life.'"

Cassie wanted to be sure Mary understood, and so she said, "Jesus was willing to leave heaven because He loves us so much that He wants us to live with Him forever. But He had to come and die for our sins so we can go to heaven."

"I still don't understand all this," said Mary. "But . . . could I go to Sir John's with you? You're so nice to me. I'd like to find some of the treasures you've found."

Cassie knew that she had discovered another treasure. She had found that she could trust God to give her courage, grace, and wisdom to show His love to someone else.

LET'S TALK

Why do you think Mary was uncomfortable when she came to Cassie's house?

What are some of the things Cassie did that showed she had good manners?

Can you think of some other gracious manners that help others to feel welcome and comfortable?

How did God say He would keep the covenant promise?

What does the name Immanuel mean?

Why would God the Father make such a wonderful promise?

Why did Jesus leave heaven and come to this earth to live among us and die for us?

What did Mary want to do because Cassie was so nice to her?

What treasure did Cassie discover?

Let's memorize God's Word: Matthew 1:23; John 3:16.

LET'S PRAY

Thank God that He loves us so much that He kept the covenant promise
and sent Jesus to live among us and die for our sins.

CHAPTER EIGHT

The Muddy Mess

CLUE #7:
Read Ephesians 2:8-9 to discover how we become
a part of God's covenant family.

For by grace you have been saved through faith. And this is not your own doing; it is the gift of God, not a result of works, so that no one may boast. (Ephesians 2:8-9)

———◼———

When Cassie woke up, she heard the soft sound of summer rain on the roof. She loved seeing how fresh and clean everything looked after a rain. *It's like God washes the whole outdoors*, she thought as she climbed out of bed.

By the time Cassie and Caleb finished breakfast and their chores, the rain had stopped. They ran outside to play. Daniel met them, and they waved to Granny Grace who was sitting on her porch reading.

"Good morning, Granny Grace," they called. "May we play in your backyard?" There were lots of trees in Granny Grace's backyard, and the children loved to play there.

"Sure," she said. "Mary and Mac are already back there."

They ran as fast as they could, and just as they got to the woods—whoosh! splat! Caleb whirled around to see Cassie crawling out of the mud. She had been so busy waving at Mary that she ran right through a huge, slippery mud puddle and lost her balance.

"Caleb," she cried, "I'm all muddy!"

"You sure are!" laughed Caleb.

"It's not funny!" Cassie moaned.

"Well, if you could see what we saw, you'd think it's funny," said Mac. "You were running full speed, and then you slipped, and your arms and legs flew straight out."

Mary added, "Then when you finally landed, mud went everywhere! Like this." To show them, Mary threw mud up in the air. But the funny thing about mud is that if you throw it up, it always comes back down. And this time, to Mac's horror, it landed right on his head. Caleb had never seen anything so funny. He was laughing so hard he could barely breathe.

"So you think that's funny," Mac laughed as he hurled a mud clod at Caleb. But Caleb ducked, and the mud clod hit Mary right in the back! So of course what happened next was the grandest mud war that had ever taken place in Granny Grace's backyard.

Finally they all fell to the ground laughing. Mary decided to go inside and get cookies and juice for everyone. She was in such a hurry that she totally forgot that she was covered with mud. She also forgot Granny Grace's rule that they were to ask permission before getting snacks.

As Mary hurriedly put cups on a tray, filled them with juice, and got a huge pile of cookies, she didn't notice that she was tracking mud everywhere. She picked up the tray and was headed outside when the cat walked through the kitchen. Mary's eyes were on the tray, and she tripped over the cat. The tray hit the floor, and cookies and juice flew all over the kitchen. Terrified, the cat screeched and jumped up on the table, knocking over the whole pitcher, spattering red juice everywhere. There was a crunching sound as the frightened cat jumped back down to the floor right onto a pile of cookies. He jumped off the cookies, onto some mud, and skidded all the way across the kitchen. The wild-eyed cat, dripping with red juice, ran toward the front door. At that very moment Mary heard the front door open and realized that Granny Grace was coming inside.

Mary panicked. She felt as if her head was spinning. She ran into the hall, opened the closet door, and hid! It was dark, but she didn't care. She was so afraid and ashamed. She sat on the floor, buried her muddy head in her hands, and sobbed.

Well, it didn't take Granny Grace long to figure out what had happened. Muddy footprints led right to the closet door. But what she did next certainly surprised Mary.

Early that morning, before Mary and Mac were up, Granny Grace had asked the Lord to show her some way to help the children understand about His love and His grace. When she saw the disaster in her kitchen, she knew that the Lord had answered her prayer.

"Oh my," she said in a gentle voice but loud enough for someone hiding in the closet to hear. "There's quite a catastrophe in my kitchen." She quickly cleaned up the entire mess. Then she walked to the closet door and opened it. She knelt down and gave Mary a big hug.

"How did you find me?" sobbed Mary.

"It wasn't too hard," replied Granny Grace. "I just followed your tracks."

"Oooh," groaned Mary. "I'm so sorry. What are you going to do to me?"

"I'm going to love you and comfort you and then help you prepare a snack for your friends." Granny Grace took Mary's hand and led her into the kitchen.

"You cleaned up the mess I made. You came and found me, and you didn't punish me," said Mary softly. "Why?"

Granny Grace began washing the mud off Mary. "Mary, I'm a sinner. I deserve to be punished for my sin. But Jesus was punished for me, and then He found me and saved me because

He loves me. I hope that what I did for you will help you to begin to understand how much God loves *you*."

"But I was so bad. How can you love me? How can God love me?" asked Mary.

Granny Grace smiled. "Mary, God doesn't love us because we're good. We can't be good enough to earn His love. We don't deserve His love. We're saved because of His grace."

"That's just like your name," observed Mary.

"Indeed it is," said Granny Grace. "My mother and daddy were so grateful for God's grace that they named me Grace. Look at this Bible verse that they taught me when I was a little girl." She picked up her Bible and read: "'For by grace you have been saved through faith. And this is not your own doing; it is the gift of God, not a result of works, so that no one may boast' (Ephesians 2:8-9)."

"But what is grace?" asked Mary.

"Grace is God's love that we can't earn and that we don't deserve. It is a gift God gives to us."

"I like that verse, Granny Grace," said Mary. "Will you help me memorize it?"

"I certainly will," said Granny Grace as she gave Mary a hug. "Now let's get some juice and cookies for everyone."

When Mary had been hiding in the closet, she had felt as if the whole world was on top of her. But as she and Granny Grace walked outside with the food, she felt as light as a feather. She felt happy. She felt loved.

Later that afternoon Mary saw Cassie sitting on her porch, and she ran over to see her. "Are you working on your journal?" she asked.

"Yes," said Cassie. "Come look at the next clue." Cassie read Clue #7: "'Look up Ephesians 2:8-9 to discover how we become a part of God's covenant family.'"

"Ephesians 2:8-9!" gasped an astonished Mary. "Cassie, that's the verse Granny Grace is helping me memorize."

LET'S TALK

What happened when the children ran into Granny Grace's backyard?

What happened when Mary went inside to get refreshments?

Why did Mary feel so miserable when she was hiding in the closet?

Why did Granny Grace clean the kitchen and then find Mary and love and comfort her?

What is grace?

Let's memorize God's Word: Ephesians 2:8-9.

LET'S PRAY

Thank God for His grace that you cannot earn and do not deserve.
Thank Him for the gift of salvation.

GLORY STORIES FROM GENESIS

CHAPTER NINE

Glory Story—Creation

GENESIS 1

TREASURE OF WISDOM AND KNOWLEDGE: God is the glorious Creator.
COVENANT VALUE: God's Glory

So whether you eat or drink or whatever you do, do it all for the glory of God.
(1 Corinthians 10:31)

———■———

When Mac heard that Mary was going to Sir John's, he decided he would go too. He acted a bit cocky about it. He said he was bored and didn't have anything else to do, but Cassie, Caleb, and Daniel suspected that he was curious to see what it was all about.

Miss Jenny and Sir John welcomed the children. Daniel turned to Mary and Mac. "That delicious smell is Miss Jenny's yummy shortbread. She makes the best shortbread in the whole world." Remember that Daniel is the charmer. And the truth is, he charmed the socks off Miss Jenny.

"Mary and Mac, this is a perfect day for you to join us," said Sir John as he gave them each a journal. "Today our adventure is going to take us back to the beginning—the very beginning. We're going to discover treasures of wisdom and knowledge about God. These treasures are in the Old Testament book of Genesis." Sir John showed the children his Bible as he explained, "The Old Testament was written before Jesus came into the world, but it tells us about Him. Genesis is the first book of the Bible. Now get comfortable, close your eyes, and try to imagine . . ."

The children could feel the wonder in Sir John's voice. "The Bible tells us that everything was dark and empty and without shape. Then the dark emptiness was shattered when God said, 'Let there be light!' And there was light. God just *spoke*, and it happened. Did you know that the Bible says we will not need a light in heaven? Cassie, will you read Revelation 21:23 for us?"

Cassie was startled. She opened her eyes and said, "Oh, sure, Sir John." She grinned sheepishly. "I think I was back at the beginning." She opened her Bible and read: "'And the city has no need of sun or moon to shine on it, for the glory of God gives it light . . .'"

"This verse is describing heaven," said Sir John. "So why won't we need the sun or moon in heaven?"

Mary had been listening intently, and she blurted out, "The glory of God will give it light!"

Sir John's eyebrows hung over his glasses. "What a fine scholar you are, lassie!" he exclaimed. "You're beginning to discover the treasures."

Sir John was quiet for a few moments. The children were sure that he was thinking about heaven. Then he continued, "After God created light, He spoke and brought everything else into existence: the sky, the water and the dry ground, plants and trees, the sun and moon, sea creatures and birds, and animals.

"God created it all in six days. Daniel, read Psalm 19:1 to discover what creation tells us about God."

Daniel read, "'The heavens declare the glory of God, and the sky above proclaims his handiwork.'" He looked up and said, "I get it. When we look at what God made, we see His glory!"

Sir John smiled, "Yes, lad . . . When we look at the sizzling sun, the shimmering stars, the majestic mountains, the towering trees, the dazzling daffodils, a hilarious hippopotamus or a beautiful butterfly. . . we should stop and listen. Listen carefully—not with our ears, but with our hearts. They are telling us about our glorious, majestic, Creator God. At the end of each day, God looked at His creation and said, 'It is good!' Creation was good because the Creator is good."

Once again there was that sweet

silence, and the children knew that Sir John was thinking about God's goodness.

After a few moments Daniel asked, "Sir John, I've been wondering . . . who made God? Where did He come from?"

"Ah, lad," said Sir John. "I like a curious mind, and I have the answer for you. No one made God. There was never a time when God did not exist. We cannot understand this, but we know it's true because the Bible tells us so. God always has been, and He always will be. After God commanded everything into existence, He said, 'Let us make man in our image, in our likeness.' What is an image?"

"I know!" exclaimed Daniel. "We talked about this in Sunday school. It's like a picture or a reflection of something else."

"Exactly," said Sir John. "If you look in a mirror, that's not really you. It's a reflection or an image of you. An image does not tell *everything* about you, but it does tell some things. The man and woman God made were not exactly like God, but they were an image of Him, and so they had a very special relationship with Him. They could know Him and talk with Him and love Him and worship Him. When God made the man and woman, He did not just say, 'It is good.' He said, 'It is *very* good.'"

Mac was shaking his head. "Wait a minute. I'm confused. I thought there was a big explosion, and then some little molecules kept evolving until after millions of years there was an ape, and finally the apes became people. Are you saying that God created everything?"

"Yes, Mac," said Sir John. "Just look about you, lad. Look at your hand. Look at your sister's eyes. Think about the birds and flowers. Do you think anything this wonderful and complicated and beautiful could have happened by accident? Oh no. A glorious Creator designed it all."

"You know," said Mac softly, "what you say makes sense."

"I think you're beginning to discover some of the treasures," Sir John told him. "Now, children, I want you to discover a covenant value—something that should be important to God's people because He is our glorious Creator."

"Umm," said Cassie as she opened her journal. "Will these clues help us find the answer?"

"Yes indeed, lassie, and that is your adventure for next week. But now it's time for us to introduce Mary and Mac to Miss Jenny's shortbread."

LET'S TALK

Why won't we need the sun or moon in heaven?

What does creation tell us about?

God made man and woman in His own image. What is an image?

What did God say when He made the man and woman?

Why was creation good?

What did you learn about God in this story?

What is the treasure of wisdom and knowledge?

Let's memorize God's Word: 1 Corinthians 10:31.

LET'S PRAY

Thank God that He is our glorious Creator King.
Ask Him to help you glorify Him in all you do.

CHAPTER TEN

Reflecting God's Glory

TREASURE OF WISDOM AND KNOWLEDGE: God is the glorious Creator.
COVENANT VALUE: God's Glory

So whether you eat or drink or whatever you do, do it all for the glory of God.
(1 Corinthians 10:31)

———■———

"Ow!" cried Cassie. "What's the deal?"

"The *deal*," snapped Caleb, "is that I want to sit by the window."

"Mom," pleaded Cassie, "tell Caleb to stop shoving!"

"I'm not *doing* anything," growled Caleb. "I'm tired, and I'm hungry, and I just want to sit where I won't be cramped."

Cassie and Caleb had spent the day at the amusement park with Daniel, Mary, and Mac. They had enjoyed a day full of rides, games, and cotton candy, but they were all tired and cranky as they piled into the van for the drive home.

"Caleb," said his mother in a soft but firm voice, "whether you eat, or drink, or when you are tired and hungry . . . " That was all she said, but she didn't need to say anything else.

Caleb put his head in his hands. He knew his mother was right. He hated it when he was tired, hungry, grumpy, and *wrong*. His mind went back to family devotions the night before. His mother had asked him and his sister a question.

"What did you learn at Sir John's today?"

"We learned that God is the glorious Creator," Cassie replied.

Caleb opened his journal and showed it to his parents. "Sir John gave us some clues to help us discover a covenant value for God's covenant children."

Their mom looked at Cassie's journal. "Okay, kids," she said, "get your Bibles and look up the clues."

Cassie read the first clue. "Isaiah 43:1, 4, 7: 'But now thus says the Lord, he who created you . . . "Fear not, for I have redeemed you; I have called you by name, you are mine. . . . you are precious in my eyes, and honored, and I love you. . . . everyone who is called by my name, whom I created for my glory, whom I formed and made."'"

Caleb read the second clue. "1 Corinthians 10:31: 'So whether you eat or drink or whatever you do, do it all for the glory of God.'" He waved his Bible excitedly. "I've got it!" he shouted.

"Me too!" squealed Cassie in her squeaky, excited voice.

"It's God's glory!" they both exclaimed at the same time.

Cassie and Caleb jumped up and did their victory dance. "Hey, you two," laughed their dad, "let's talk about this. Do you know what it means to glorify God?"

"Sort of," said Cassie. "But I don't know how to explain it."

"Let me see if I can help you," Dad offered. "God's glory is the beauty and goodness of His character. We glorify Him when we reflect His character. Do you know what reflect means?"

Caleb scratched his head. "We've been studying about the moon reflecting the light from the sun. Is that the same thing?"

"Bingo!" said his dad. "That's the perfect example. How much light does the moon have?"

"None," said Caleb. "The light we see is the reflection of the sun's light bouncing off the moon."

"Exactly. Now, my young astronomer, why do we sometimes see a full moon and sometimes just a little sliver of the moon?"

Caleb could hardly wait to answer. He loved books about the solar system, and he loved to talk about it. "It all depends on the position of the moon as it travels around the earth," he explained. "The position of the moon determines how much of it reflects sunlight to earth."

"So," asked his dad, "what does all of this teach us about reflecting the light of God's glory?"

"I think I understand," Caleb said, intrigued. "We are like the moon. We have no light of our own. And I guess we have to be in the right position to reflect God's glory."

Cassie stared at her brother in wonder. "That is so cool," she said.

Their dad wanted to be sure they understood. "You see," he explained, "when we are in a right relationship with the Lord Jesus, we will reflect His glory. We will be more and more like Him. We will show His goodness. What do you think moves us away from the right position to reflect His glory?"

"I'm not sure," answered Cassie, "but I'll bet it's sin."

"Bingo again!" said their dad. "So when we sin, we must quickly ask God to forgive us so that we get back in the right position to reflect His glory. And remember, 1 Corinthians 10:31 says that we are to glorify God in everything we do. In our work and in our play, in how we worship God and in how we treat others, in what we think and what we say—in all of life we are to glorify God."

As Caleb sat in the backseat of the van remembering the night before, he could almost hear his dad's voice again. "When we sin, we must quickly ask God to forgive us . . ." Caleb prayed in his heart, *Dear Lord, forgive me for getting in the wrong position. Forgive me for being selfish. Help me to glorify You.*

Caleb knew what he should do next, and he didn't waste a minute. "Cassie," he said, "I'm sorry I shoved you. And Mary, Mac, and Daniel, I'm sorry. Will you forgive me too?"

"Why are you apologizing to us?" asked Mac.

"Yeah, you didn't shove any of us," added Mary.

"I think I did something worse than shove you," Caleb explained. "I didn't reflect God's glory to you. I'm really sorry."

Mac had a bewildered look on his face. "You guys are really different."

"You're right, Mac," agreed Mary softly. "They're different from any friends we've ever had."

Daniel, the charmer, never at a loss for words, grinned. "I'm going to take that as a compliment," he said.

The kids all laughed, but Caleb's mom prayed in her heart, *Dear Lord, thank You for giving Caleb the grace to glorify You.*

LET'S TALK

Why was Caleb so grumpy?

Since God is the Creator King, what is a covenant value for covenant kids?

What does it mean to reflect God's glory?

What gets us out of position so that we don't reflect God's glory?

When Caleb realized that he was out of that position, what did he do?

When and where are we to glorify God?

Let's memorize God's Word: 1 Corinthians 10:31.

LET'S PRAY

Ask God for grace to glorify Him in everything you do.

CHAPTER ELEVEN

Mary Believes

TREASURE OF WISDOM AND KNOWLEDGE: God is the glorious Creator.
COVENANT VALUE: God's Glory

*So whether you eat or drink or whatever you do, do it all for the glory of God.
(1 Corinthians 10:31)*

Cassie was excited. Susie was coming to spend the day. Susie's family had been on vacation, and Cassie had not seen her for two weeks.

When Susie arrived, the girls went to the kitchen for a snack. They could hardly eat for chattering. Susie told Cassie about her vacation, and Cassie told Susie about Sir John and Mary and Mac. "Look at my journal," Cassie urged. "We discover some of the treasures about who God is, and then we find a covenant value. That's something that should be very important to God's covenant children. See. Look at this page. We learned that since God is our glorious Creator, we should reflect His glory."

Then Cassie said the memory verse for Susie. "First Corinthians 10:31: 'So whether you eat or drink or whatever you do, do it all for the glory of God.'"

"Well," grinned Susie, "are we glorifying God as we eat our snack?"

"It all depends," laughed Cassie's mom. "Do you have a grateful heart, and are you being polite and gracious?"

The girls quickly sat up straight, put one hand in their laps, and Susie said in a very grown-up voice, "This snack is so delicious. Thank you very much."

The girls giggled as Cassie's mom tickled them. "You two are so funny."

"Stop! Okay. Enough," squealed Cassie. Then she turned to Susie. "Let's go play with our dolls. Whether we eat or drink or play with our dolls, we'll do it for God's glory." Cassie and Susie had dolls just alike, and they loved to pretend they were bathing and dressing and caring for their babies.

Just then the doorbell rang. Cassie opened the door to find Mary standing there.

"Hi, Cassie. Do you want to play?"

Now if we could have gotten inside those three girls' heads at that moment, this is what we would have heard:

Susie was thinking: *Oh no, I don't want to share my doll or my friend with someone else. It'll spoil our fun if Cassie invites her to play.*

Mary was thinking: *Oh no, Susie is here. She's Cassie's best friend. I'm sure they won't let me play.*

Cassie was thinking: *Oh my, I want to show Mary God's glory, but it has been so long since Susie and I played together. I really don't want someone else here. But wait a minute—it's not about what I want. It's about glorifying God. Dear Jesus, please help me.*

Well, Jesus did help Cassie, and He helped Susie. When Susie heard Cassie say, "I'm glad you came over, Mary. Susie is spending the day with me. We're going to play with our dolls, but it'll be more fun if you play with us," Susie knew that Cassie was glorifying God. She prayed in her heart that the Lord would help her to be kind. "Hi, Mary, I'm glad you're going to play with us," she said.

The girls laughed and played and had a great time. Cassie's mom invited Mary to join them for lunch. When Cassie said the blessing, she thanked the Lord for Susie and Mary. Then she thanked Him for the food.

Mary was quiet for a moment. Then she said, "You two really are different. Is it because you have discovered the treasures that Sir John talks about?"

Susie wasn't sure what to say, but Cassie got right to the point. "Mary, Jesus is our Savior. He died for our sins, and He lives in our hearts. The only reason we're different is because He helps us to live for His glory."

"Will Jesus be my Savior too?" asked Mary.

"Sure He will," said Cassie and Susie at the same time.

Cassie's mom had been listening and could stay quiet no longer. "Hold everything," she blurted out as she dashed to the telephone. The three girls were speechless. They heard Cassie's mom say, "Grace, get over here quick." Cassie's mom dialed another number while the girls just stared at her. "Jenny, stop whatever you're doing and run down here."

Cassie's mom took a deep breath, turned to the girls, and said, "You girls know that every morning Grace, Jenny, and I walk together. What you don't know is that before we walk, we pray. We have a list of all the children in our church, and we pray for ten of them each morning. Mary, five years ago we started praying for you and Mac every day. We have asked the Lord to give you new hearts that will trust and obey Him. I can't let my prayer partners miss this moment."

Just then Miss Jenny came running in with a towel wrapped around her head. "This had better be good," she panted. "I just got out of the shower."

Granny Grace was right behind her. "What's wrong? Is someone hurt?" But she quickly saw that all three girls were fine.

Cassie's mom was about to burst. "Mary just asked a question, and I wanted you two to help me answer her. Mary asked if Jesus will be her Savior."

It's really hard to describe what happened next, but three startled little girls watched three grown women hug and cry and laugh. Then the three women almost smothered the little girls with hugs and kisses. Finally when things settled down a bit, a little voice said, "Well, will Jesus be my Savior?"

"Oh, Mary," wept her grandmother, "I've prayed for you since before you were born. I believed with all my heart that the Lord God chose you to be His treasured possession. I've prayed that He would give you a heart to know Him. Mary, do you believe that you are a sinner and that you need a Savior?"

Mary nodded her head, and her grandmother continued, "Do you believe that Jesus died for your sins?"

"I do," said Mary emphatically.

"My dear child," said Granny Grace, "then just ask Him to be your Savior."

They all knelt in a circle and held hands. Mary prayed, "Dear Jesus, thank You for dying for me. Please be my Savior. And please give Mac a heart to know You too."

The Bible says that there is great "joy in heaven over one sinner who repents" (Luke 15:7), but there was also great rejoicing in that kitchen when Mary asked Jesus to be her Savior.

---■---

LET'S TALK

What happened just as Cassie and Susie were ready to play with their dolls?

If we could have gotten inside each girl's head, what would we have heard them thinking?

How did Cassie glorify God?

How did Susie glorify God?

What question did Mary ask while they were eating lunch?

What did Cassie's mom do?

What had Cassie's mom, Granny Grace, and Miss Jenny been doing for five years?

Let's memorize God's Word: 1 Corinthians 10:31.

---■---

LET'S PRAY

Ask God for grace to glorify Him in everything you think and say and do.

CHAPTER TWELVE

The Birthday Gift

TREASURE OF WISDOM AND KNOWLEDGE: God is the glorious Creator.

COVENANT VALUE: God's Glory

So whether you eat or drink or whatever you do, do it all for the glory of God.
(1 Corinthians 10:31)

"I can hardly wait to hear what Sir John will teach us today," said Mary as the children walked to Sir John's house.

Mac sneered at his sister. "What in the world has happened to you? You're acting weird."

"Mac, I keep trying to tell you. I have a new heart. Jesus is my Savior," Mary patiently explained.

Mac just groaned and shook his head.

They rang the doorbell, and Miss Jenny welcomed them. She hugged all the children, and they hugged her back—except Mac. He was stiff as a board.

"Hello, lads and lassies," said Sir John as he took Mary's hand in his big wrinkled one. "My child, I heard the good news, and I thank God for answering our prayers and giving you a new heart to know Him. Today I have a very special story especially for you. It's about a young covenanter girl just about your age."

"I remember the covenanters," declared Cassie. "Their motto was 'For Christ's Crown and Covenant.'"

"Right you are," laughed Sir John. "These were the people in Scotland who said that Jesus is the King of His church. Many men and women and boys and girls suffered and died because of their faithfulness to Christ's crown and covenant."

"Is this a true story?" asked Mary.

"Yes, it is, child," replied Sir John. "It's about a girl named Janet. Her father was a covenanter. The king had forbidden the covenanters to meet together, so they met secretly to worship God even though it was very dangerous. Janet's mother loved her husband and children, but she did not know and love the Lord Jesus. She did not want her husband to go to the meetings with the covenanters. He was very patient with his wife, and he tenderly talked to her about his love for Christ's crown and covenant.

"Janet listened to her father, and soon she became a Christian too. She loved Jesus and wanted to live for His glory. She went to the meetings with her father, but this made her mother angry. Janet's mother treated her harshly, but young Janet prayed that she would show her mother God's glory.

"One day Janet's mother said, 'I think Janet's disposition is much more sweet and kind than it used to be. She seems to be the most affectionate and obedient of all our children.' Her husband said, 'The change you see in Janet is the result of the grace of God, which changes the heart and makes us new creatures. Janet receives this grace from hearing the preaching at our meetings.'"

Sir John paused, and one could have heard a pin drop. Then Caleb asked, "Well, did Janet's mother start going to the meetings with them?"

"No, lad," continued Sir John. "She became even more angry and would not let Janet go. But once, when Janet's father was in hiding from the soldiers, Janet heard about a meeting. She wanted to see her dear father, and so she went. Soon after she found her beloved father, the soldiers came, and the group quickly scattered. In the confusion, Janet and her father were separated.

"It was a long way home, but the frightened girl ran as fast as she could. When she arrived at home, her mother was furious, but Janet did not argue with her. She was not a strong girl, and she became sick. When her father got home, he knelt by her bed and prayed. Janet's mother saw her daughter's peace, and day after day she listened to her husband talk to Janet about Jesus.

"One day Janet's mother said, 'My dear child, I have been so unkind to you, and you were always so gentle with me. And now I am afraid I shall lose you.'

"'My dear mother,' replied Janet, 'I am indeed very ill, and I do not think I shall recover, but my heart is full of peace, and my trust is in the Savior. If it is His will for me to die, I long to enter into His rest. But, my dear mother, I am anxious on your account, and it would greatly lighten the affliction of my dying to see you turn to the Savior and seek His face with all your heart.'"

Once again Sir John was quiet. The children sat in silence, and finally Daniel asked, "Did Janet die?"

Sir John nodded. "Yes, but before she died, her mother trusted Jesus. Janet saw a blessed change in her mother. Janet reflected God's glory to her mother, and her mother began to reflect God's glory to Janet. The little family had sweet times together before Janet entered her heavenly rest."

The children sat very still as they thought about the story. Then Mary said softly, "I want to be faithful like Janet. I want to show my mother God's glory."

"Ah, my child," said Sir John as he reached out and drew Mary to his side, "God has given you a new heart. Now you must ask Him to show you more and more of His glory and to give you grace to reflect His glory."

"But where can I see God's glory?" asked Mary.

"I was hoping you would ask that," replied Sir John as he handed her a gaily wrapped gift. "I have a birthday present for you."

"But it's not my birthday," protested Mary. But she eagerly opened the gift anyway.

"Ah, but it is, my child. It's your spiritual birthday."

"It's a Bible," exclaimed Mary, "and it has my name on it!"

Sir John opened the Bible. "Mary, I wrote here the date that you trusted Jesus as your Savior so that you will remember your spiritual birthday. And I wrote a verse that I want you to pray whenever you read God's Word."

Mary read the verse: "'Make your face shine upon your servant, and teach me your statutes (Psalm 119:135).' What does 'statutes' mean?"

"That means the Bible," explained Sir John. "When we read the Bible, God's Spirit teaches us His ways. He shines His glory upon our hearts so that we know Him better. And the more we learn of Him, the more we will reflect His glory."

"Oh, Sir John," cried Mary as she gave the old gentleman a hug, "this is the best present I ever got."

The other children crowded around Mary to see her new Bible—well, everyone except Mac. He just sat on the couch and shook his head.

LET'S TALK

What did you learn from the story about Janet?

What are some of the things Janet's mother noticed about her?

What did Sir John give Mary?

Why did he give her a gift?

What happens when we read God's Word?

What is the treasure of wisdom and knowledge in this story?

What is the covenant value here?

Let's memorize God's Word: 1 Corinthians 10:31.

LET'S PRAY

Ask God to make His face shine upon you and to give you grace to reflect His glory.

This story was adapted from an old book I found in London, *Select Extracts for the Young,* issued by the committee of the General Assembly of the Free Church of Scotland, for the publication of the works of Scottish Reformers and Divines.

CHAPTER THIRTEEN

Glory Story— God Puts People in Charge

GENESIS 1

TREASURE OF WISDOM AND KNOWLEDGE: God is the King of creation.

COVENANT VALUE: Stewardship

As each one has received a gift, minister it to one another, as good stewards of the manifold grace of God. (1 Peter 4:10 NKJV)

"Hello, lads and lassies," Sir John greeted the children. "Miss Jenny is quite busy today. She's making extra batches of shortbread."

The children followed him to the library. "Why is she making extra?" asked Daniel with a gleam in his eyes. It did not take a detective to know that he was hoping it meant more shortbread for him.

"There's plenty for you, my little charmer," said Miss Jenny as she peeped out from the kitchen. "But I'm making extra for some teenage girls who are coming this afternoon. Hunter, the youth pastor at our church, asked me to be a spiritual mother to these girls."

"Don't they have mothers?" asked Mary.

Miss Jenny smiled. "Yes, Mary, they have mothers, but it's good for them to have other women in the covenant community who love and teach them. I was surprised when Hunter asked me to do this. I didn't think young girls would want to spend time with someone as old as I am."

"Miss Jenny, anyone would love to spend time with you." Now I'm sure you know who said this. Of course—it was that charmer, Daniel.

"I have a question," piped up Mary. "Why do *you* want to spend time with kids like us and with teenage girls? And why do you take the time to bake cookies for us? Wouldn't you rather do things for yourself?"

"Ah, lassie," Sir John replied smiling, "you have asked a very important question, and our story for today will help you to know the answer. After God created everything, He said, 'Let us make man in our image.' He created the man and the woman in His image so that they could know Him and even be something like Him. He gave them something that no other creature in all of creation had—God gave them souls. We can't see our soul, but it is the gift God gave us so that we can worship and serve Him. He created us in His image so that we can reflect His glory."

"Sir John, what is God's glory?" asked Mary.

"Excellent question, lassie. God's glory is the light and the brilliance of His presence. It is His goodness and truth and love and kindness. It is His character."

"I like these stories about God's glory," Mary declared.

"Yeah," grinned Cassie. "I like these glory stories!"

"Glory stories . . . I like that!" exclaimed Sir John. "Now, my young scholars, let's get to work and discover another treasure of wisdom and knowledge about God."

The children eagerly opened their journals. Daniel read the clue: "'Look up Genesis 1:28 to discover what God told the man and woman to do.'"

The children were surprised when Mac said, "I'll read it." He hadn't brought a Bible, so he looked on with Caleb. "'And God blessed them. And God said to them, "Be fruitful and multiply and fill the earth and subdue it and have dominion over the fish of the sea and over the birds of the heavens and over every living thing that moves on the earth."'"

"God told them to be fruitful and multiply," said Cassie. "Does that mean they were to have children?"

"Yes, it does," answered Sir John. "And what else did God tell them to do? Get out your spiritual spyglasses."

Mary looked at her Bible and read, "'Have dominion over the fish of the sea and over the birds of the heavens and over every living thing that moves on the earth.' What does that mean, Sir John?"

"Well, lassie, it means that God is the King of His creation. Our Creator King said that people are to rule the earth for Him. We are to manage His world for His glory and for the good of others. Our covenant value is stewardship."

"Stewart's ship?" asked Cassie. "What does a ship that belongs to a guy named Stewart have to do with a covenant value?"

Sir John exploded in laughter. In fact, the children thought he was going to roll out of his chair laughing. He gasped, "You children . . . are so wonderful. . . . You make this old man laugh. . . . I love being with you!"

The children had no idea what was so funny, but they got tickled watching Sir John laugh, and soon they were laughing so hard you could hear their squeals in the kitchen. Miss Jenny came running in to see what the hullabaloo was about, and she started chuckling as loudly as everyone else. That's how it is with laughter. Sometimes you don't even have to know what's funny; you just join in the fun. When Sir John finally got his breath and told Miss Jenny about "Stewart's ship," the laughter started all over. Miss Jenny had tears rolling down her cheeks she was laughing so hard.

Finally they all quieted down, and Caleb asked, "Now explain why we were all laughing our heads off. What was so funny?"

Sir John took a big handkerchief from his pocket and wiped his glasses. "My young scholars, a steward is a manager. It's someone who takes care of something that belongs to someone else. Stewardship means that we are being good managers."

"Ooh," the children all said at once.

"Actually, Cassie," admitted Mary, "I thought your question made perfect sense."

"Yes, it did," agreed Sir John. "And it showed a great deal of creative thinking. Now there is a clue in your journal that I want you to think about before next week. This clue will help you learn about being good stewards of the grace God has given you."

Mary scrunched up her face as if thinking really hard. "But I still don't understand why you and Miss Jenny spend time with us rather than just doing what *you* enjoy," she said.

"I think I know," declared Caleb. "When you and Miss Jenny teach us, you are being good stewards of the things God has taught you."

"Right you are, my lad," proclaimed Sir John.

Now it was Daniel's turn, and to no one's surprise his comment had to do with shortbread. "And Miss Jenny is a good steward of her ability to make shortbread because she shares it with others!"

Sir John laughed out loud. "And I suppose you're ready and willing to let her share it with you," he said as they adjourned to the kitchen.

———■———

LET'S TALK

Why did Miss Jenny make extra batches of shortbread?

What did God give human beings that the animals do not have?

Read Genesis 1:28. What did God tell the man and woman to do?

What is the treasure of wisdom and knowledge that we learn about God in this story?

What is the covenant value?

What is a steward?

Let's memorize God's Word: 1 Peter 4:10.

———■———

LET'S PRAY

Thank God that He is the Creator King.

Ask Him to help you to be a good steward of everything He gives you.

CHAPTER FOURTEEN

A Faithful Dude

Treasure of wisdom and knowledge: God is the King of creation.
Covenant Value: Stewardship

As each one has received a gift, minister it to one another, as good stewards of the manifold grace of God. (1 Peter 4:10 NKJV)

———■———

"Did everyone answer the questions?" Caleb asked as the children walked to Sir John's house.

"I answered the first one, but I couldn't figure out what the second one meant," replied Daniel.

"Me either," said Cassie and Mary at the same time.

"That one stumped me too," admitted Caleb.

Mac just shrugged and tried to act cool.

When the children were settled in Sir John's library, he looked at them with a twinkle in his eyes. "Would you like to hear a story about John Knox?"

"Sure," they all said. Well, everyone except Mac. He looked bored and uninterested.

"John Knox's call to be a minister of the Gospel was most unusual. A group of people who believed God's Word lived together in the castle at St. Andrews in Scotland because it was a safe place for them. John Knox and some boys he tutored were part of the group."

"Do you mean the boys lived at the castle?" asked Cassie.

Sir John nodded.

"Cool." Daniel grinned. "Just think—swords and shields and a moat around the castle and adventures and—"

"Okay," laughed Sir John. "Back to our story. Every day John Knox taught the boys their lessons, and every day they went to the chapel in the castle, and he taught them from the Gospel of John. The man who preached for the people in the castle tried to get John Knox to be the preacher, but he refused because he didn't think God was calling him to be a preacher. However, everyone else thought that God had given him the gift of preaching. One Sunday during the sermon, the preacher looked at John Knox and said, 'Brother, in the name of God and of His Son Jesus Christ, I charge you not to refuse this holy vocation.' (A vocation is the work people do, like their career.) The preacher then asked the congregation if they wanted John Knox to be their preacher, and they all said that they did. Well, John Knox burst into tears. And that's how he became a preacher."

"Why did he burst into tears?" quizzed Daniel.

"I think he was overcome with the privilege and the responsibility of being a minister of the Gospel," explained Sir John. "God gave John Knox the gift of preaching, and he was a good steward of that gift. He became a brave and faithful preacher of God's Word. But shortly after that, a dreadful thing happened."

"What?" the children all asked. Well, everyone except Mac. He was still trying to act bored.

"An army attacked the castle. The people inside were captured and put on a ship where they were forced to do the terribly hard work of rowing the boat."

"Was it Stewart's ship?" asked Caleb with a playful grin.

Sir John smiled. "Clever," he said and then continued, "They were kept as prisoners for two years, but John Knox did not give up hope, and he encouraged the others to remain faithful. Once when the ship was off the coast of Scotland, one of the prisoners pointed to the steeples of St. Andrews and asked Knox if he had ever been there. Children, let me read his answer to you."

There were tears in Sir John's eyes as he picked up a book and read the words of John Knox: "'Yes, I know it well . . . and I am fully persuaded, how weak so ever I now appear, that I shall not depart this life, till that my tongue shall glorify his godly name in the same place.'"

Sir John was quiet. Finally everyone was startled when Mac asked impatiently, "Well? Did he ever preach there again?"

"Yes, lad, he did," replied Sir John softly. "Several years later he returned to Scotland as a free man. He was determined to preach in St. Andrews. But the authorities said that if John Knox came there, he would be welcomed by a twelve-gun salute, and that most of it would light upon his nose!"

"You mean they threatened to kill him?" asked Mac. "What did he do?"

"His friends tried to persuade him not to go," answered Sir John. "But John Knox said, 'My life is in the custody of Him whose glory I seek.' He preached, and nothing happened to him."

"He was one brave dude," declared Mac.

"Yes, but more than that, he was a faithful dude," laughed Sir John. "Whether he was standing in a pulpit or laboring as a prisoner on a ship, he was a good steward of God's grace. Now, my friends, let's talk about the first question in your journals. What are some of the gifts God has given you? Who would like to read your answer?"

"I will," offered Mary. "God has given me a new heart, and He has given me new friends."

"He has given us the Bible and Jesus," said Daniel.

"And our families," added Cassie.

"Excellent, excellent," said Sir John. "Now let's look at the next question: 'How do we minister our gifts to one another?' Who would like to answer this question?"

"To tell you the truth, Sir John," admitted Caleb, "that question stumped us all."

"Not me. I think I know the answer," announced Mac. Four heads turned so fast they almost got whiplash, and eight eyes almost popped out of their sockets. Only Sir John seemed not at all surprised. "Well, lad," he urged, "why don't you explain it to the others."

"It's just like John Knox. God gave him the gift to preach, and he used it to help the people in the castle and the people on that ship. You're supposed to use whatever gifts God gives you to help others."

"Outstanding!" exclaimed Sir John. "You see, children, our God is such a wise and loving King that He planned exactly what He wants done and who will do it. He designed each of us in a specific way to do specific things. He gives us abilities and skills and opportunities, and we are to be good stewards of all that He gives us."

Mac was stunned. "This Christian stuff is really big," he said as he shook his head.

LET'S TALK

How did John Knox become a preacher?

What happened when an army captured the castle?

Did John Knox ever preach again?

What are some of the gifts God has given you?

How do we use our gifts to help one another?

Why do you have the abilities and opportunities you have?

*Why do you live in the place on the planet and
at the time in history that you do?*

Let's memorize God's Word: 1 Peter 4:10.

LET'S PRAY

Thank God that He is the King of creation.
Ask Him to help you to be a good steward of everything He gives you.

The information for this story is from *For Kirk and Covenant: The Stalwart Courage of John Knox* by Douglas Wilson.

CHAPTER FIFTEEN

A Good Joke

TREASURE OF WISDOM AND KNOWLEDGE: God is the King of creation.

COVENANT VALUE: Stewardship

As each one has received a gift, minister it to one another, as good stewards of the manifold grace of God. (1 Peter 4:10 NKJV)

Caleb was riding his scooter when he saw Sir John out for his daily walk. "Hi, Sir John. What's new with you?"

Sir John waved. "Well, laddie, at my age few things are new. But I did hear a new joke. Would you like to hear it?"

"Sure," said Caleb as he pushed his scooter and walked alongside the old gentleman.

Sir John loved to tell jokes, and usually they were so corny they were funny. But the funniest part was watching him laugh at his own jokes.

"When do you stop at green and go at red?" he asked.

"Okay, I give up," replied Caleb.

"When you're eating a watermelon!" said Sir John with great glee. "Now I have another one. How do you shoot a purple elephant?"

"I have no idea." Caleb grinned.

"With a purple elephant gun!" Sir John laughed. He paused for effect and then continued, "How do you shoot a pink elephant?"

"I suppose with a *pink* elephant gun," answered Caleb.

"No! You squeeze his trunk until he turns purple, and then

you shoot him with the purple elephant gun!" Sir John could hardly get the last words out because he was roaring with laughter.

Just then they passed Caleb's house, and Caleb heard Cassie calling him from their backyard. "Sir John, shh! Don't be so loud!" he whispered.

"What? What's wrong? Why are we whispering?"

"So she won't hear us," replied Caleb.

Sir John was still laughing at his joke, so he had a difficult time being quiet. "So who doesn't hear us?" he asked.

"Cassie," answered Caleb.

"Cassie?" questioned Sir John rather loudly.

"Shh!!"

"I don't understand."

Caleb took a deep breath and whispered, "I don't want Cassie to hear us talking."

"I understand that. What I don't understand is *why* you don't want Cassie to hear us," responded Sir John.

"Because she has been pestering me all day, and I don't want her to know where I am," replied Caleb.

Just then they heard Cassie coming around to the front yard. "Caleb, Caleb, is that you?" she called.

"Uh oh! I gotta go!" Caleb sped off on his scooter.

"Hi, Sir John," called Cassie. "Have you seen Caleb? I thought I heard him."

"Yes, lassie. He was here, but he rode off on his scooter. Why are you looking for him?"

"I need him to fix my doll," replied Cassie.

"What's wrong with your doll?" asked Sir John.

"Well, look." Cassie held up a pitiful-looking doll. "Her nose fell off, and she looks really funny without it. I need Caleb to glue Miss Molly's nose back on. I would do it myself, but Mom won't let me use the super glue anymore 'cause last time I accidentally glued my hands together."

"Umm, that could present a problem," remarked Sir John. "If I see Caleb, I'll tell him you're looking for him."

"Thanks," said Cassie.

Sir John got to his house and sat down in his front-porch rocker. Miss Jenny brought a pitcher of lemonade, and he asked her for an extra glass. A few minutes later Caleb coasted by. "Hello, laddie, come and join me for some lemonade."

"Sure," said Caleb. He was a little surprised that there was already a glass for him. "You were waiting for me, weren't you?" asked Caleb. "This is about me hiding from Cassie, isn't it? And I'll bet it has something to do with 'Stewart's ship,'" he said rather sheepishly.

"What a clever one you are." Sir John smiled. "What do you think stewardship has to do with your little sister?"

"Well," said Caleb as he took a big gulp of lemonade, "I'm supposed to be a good steward of everything God gives me, and He gave me a little sister—right?"

"Keep going, my young thinker," urged Sir John.

Caleb put his head in his hands. "But, Sir John, she really gets on my nerves sometimes. I guess I know what I'm supposed to do, but I just don't want to do it."

"Now we're getting somewhere," declared the old gentleman. "Caleb, you are very close to discovering a treasure. Now think about our clues. What is the covenant promise?"

Caleb recited 2 Corinthians 6:16 slowly: "'I will make my dwelling among them and walk among them, and I will be their God, and they shall be my people.'" He scratched his head. "But how does that help me to be a good steward of my little sister?"

"Keep thinking," instructed Sir John. "How does God make us willing and able to believe the covenant promise and to live for Christ's crown and covenant?"

Caleb recited Jeremiah 24:7: "'I will give them a heart to know that I am the LORD, and they shall be my people and I will be their God.'"

"Caleb," said Sir John, "the glorious Creator, the King of the universe, is *your* God. He has given you a heart to know Him. His Holy Spirit lives in you. He will give you the power to become more and more like Him and to reflect His glory."

The old man and the young boy sat quietly for a few minutes. Finally Caleb said slowly, "I think I'm starting to get it."

"Keep thinking, my boy," said Sir John.

Caleb was still thinking even as he began speaking. "When I know what I'm supposed to do . . . and don't want to do it . . . I can ask God to help me." Suddenly Caleb's whole face turned into a huge smile as he continued enthusiastically, "And He will because He is my God, and I am His child, and He lives in me! I do see, Sir John! God will change me so that I will *want* to do what He tells me to do."

"Oh, lad, you've discovered a precious treasure!" exclaimed Sir John.

"Caleb! There you are," called a squeaky voice. "I've been looking everywhere for you. Will you help me?"

"Hi, Cassie. Sure, I'll help you. What's the problem?"

"Miss Molly's nose fell off, and I need you to glue it back on."

Caleb laughed. "Okay. I'd hate to see you glue your hands together again."

As the children walked away, Sir John called, "Caleb, 'Stewart's ship' is looking fine today."

"Now that's a good joke," laughed Caleb.

LET'S TALK

Why was Caleb hiding from Cassie?

*What does stewardship have to do with having a little sister,
or big brother, or parent, or friend?*

*What has God given us so that we can know Him
and learn to obey Him?*

What should we do when we don't want to obey Him?

Let's memorize God's Word: 1 Peter 4:10.

LET'S PRAY

Thank God that He is the King of creation.
Ask Him to help you to be a good steward of all the people He puts in your life.

CHAPTER SIXTEEN

A Lot to Learn

TREASURE OF WISDOM AND KNOWLEDGE: God is the King of creation.

COVENANT VALUE: Stewardship

As each one has received a gift, minister it to one another, as good stewards of the manifold grace of God. (1 Peter 4:10 NKJV)

———■———

"Cassie, will you get the mail for me?" requested her mom.

"Sure," replied Cassie. When she walked out to the mailbox, she noticed cars and people everywhere. Then Cassie realized that the people were teenagers from her church. She could see some of them washing windows at Granny Grace's house and some working in the yard at Sir John's. She ran back inside with the mail. "Mom, what are all the teenagers from our church doing?"

"This is the Saturday Hunter planned for the youth group to do some work for the elderly and the widows in our church," she answered.

"Hunter is really cool. May we go help?" asked Caleb.

"Sure," said his mom.

Cassie and Caleb ran outside and found Hunter carrying a ladder into a neighbor's yard. "Hey, Hunter, may we help?"

"Sure, come with me. I'm going to clean gutters, and I need someone to pick up the trash I throw down."

"Why are you and the youth group doing all this work?" Caleb asked as they put leaves and sticks into big trash bags.

"Well," explained Hunter, "our elderly members and our widows are part of our church family. God tells us to love and care for each other. He has given these teenagers the gift of strong, healthy bodies. One way they can use that gift is to help our older members with chores that are hard for them to do."

"Umm," said Caleb. "So they're being good stewards of their healthy bodies."

"Hey, that's right," said Hunter. "You're quite a thinker."

"We have a good teacher," remarked Caleb.

"And who would that be?"

"Sir John," answered Cassie and Caleb together.

When all the work was done, the children saw Hunter standing beside his car talking to Mac. Hunter had a really, really cool car with bike racks on top. All the kids knew that he had two mountain bikes—one for himself and one to take guys in the youth group out to ride the dirt tracks. Caleb could hardly wait until he would be old enough for the youth group. As they walked by, they heard Hunter say to Mac, "Okay, I'll pick you up this afternoon, and we'll go ride."

Anger swept over Caleb. He walked into his house and straight to his dad. "I just don't get it," he said. "Why does Mac get to go ride with Hunter, and he's not even in the youth group? It's not fair."

"Actually there's a really good explanation for that," replied his dad. "The elders have asked Hunter to spend time with boys in our church family who don't have dads. Hunter is just trying to minister to Mac."

It was as if someone had thrown cold water on Caleb. He was stunned.

"Dad, I keep messing up," he moaned. "I wasn't even thinking about Hunter using his bike to help Mac. I was just thinking about myself. I don't think I'll ever learn about being a good steward of the gifts God gives."

"Well, son, there's a lot to learn. Don't get discouraged. I'm thankful that you're thinking about stewardship. Just keep praying, and the Lord will help you."

The next morning at church Caleb went by the playground before he went to his Sunday school class. He knew he didn't have time, but he wanted to go down the new slide. Well, he got mud on his hands and had to make a quick stop by the bathroom to wash. He washed his hands, grabbed a wad of paper towels, dashed out into the hall, and threw the paper towels down as he rounded the corner. Smack! He bumped into Sir John, who almost lost his balance. Caleb stumbled and ran right into a little toddler, who went sprawling and then started crying. Then Caleb bumped into Hunter, who said, "Whoa! What's going on here?"

"I'm sorry," panted Caleb. "I was in a hurry." Hunter and Caleb checked on Sir John and the toddler.

Then Hunter looked at Caleb and said, "Let's talk, buddy. Why were you in such a hurry?"

Caleb explained about going by the playground.

Hunter nodded. "The playground is fun—lots of fun," he said.

"Have you tried the new slide?" asked Caleb.

"Not yet," replied Hunter. "But, Caleb, do you think this was the best use of your time this morning?"

Caleb answered rather slowly. "I guess not. . . . I guess that's why I was in such a hurry."

Hunter continued, "You made a choice, and then to live with that choice, you had to rush around and cause a little bit of trouble. You could say that you weren't being a very good steward of your time."

Oh no—not Hunter too! thought Caleb to himself.

Hunter grinned. "Okay. What's that look on your face all about?"

Caleb answered, "Well, I've been hearing a lot about stewardship lately, and I'm not too good at it. Yesterday Sir John showed me that I wasn't being a good steward of my sister. And now this."

"Yeah, this stewardship thing is kind of hard sometimes, but it's very important," replied Hunter.

Caleb was glad that Hunter seemed to understand. "So I guess I wasn't being a good steward of my time this morning," he admitted. "And actually I wasn't being a good steward of our church when I threw paper towels on the floor."

"Caleb, I think you've got it!" said Hunter.

Caleb shook his head. "Well, maybe. I know it, but now I've got to do it."

Hunter laughed as he walked Caleb to his class. "You know, Caleb, you're exactly right. We're to be good stewards of every minute God gives us and of all the people and things He gives us. That *is* a lot to learn."

"Thanks for helping me, Hunter."

"Thanks for being willing to learn," replied Hunter. "God has given you a new heart, Caleb, and that's why you want to learn about being a good steward. I'm learning too, so let's pray for each other. Deal?"

"Deal!" agreed Caleb.

LET'S TALK

Why were the teenagers doing chores at Granny Grace's home and Sir John's?

What are some ways we can be good stewards of the church family God gives us?

What are some things we can do to be good stewards of the church building that God gives us?

What has God given us so that we can know Him and learn to obey Him?

Let's memorize God's Word: 1 Peter 4:10.

LET'S PRAY

Thank God that He is the Creator King.
Ask Him to help you to be a good steward of every gift He gives you.

CHAPTER SEVENTEEN

Glory Story—
The Covenant of Grace

Genesis 2—3

TREASURE OF WISDOM AND KNOWLEDGE: God is the God of grace.

COVENANT VALUE: Worship

Oh come, let us worship and bow down; let us kneel before the LORD, our Maker! For he is our God, and we are the people of his pasture, and the sheep of his hand. (Psalm 95:6-7)

———————■———————

"Well, did you have fun?" Caleb asked Mac as they walked to Sir John's house.

Caleb was surprised that there was no jealously in his heart. He had prayed a lot about it, because he had been *really* mad and *really* jealous. But now he *really* did want to hear about Mac's time with Hunter.

"Oooh yeah!" exclaimed Mac. "It was so cool."

Caleb noticed that Mac was much friendlier today. When they got to Sir John's, Mac seemed glad to be there. "Hi, Sir John," said the children as they filed into the library.

Before they even sat down, Mac said, "I have an announcement." Everyone got very quiet. "When I went bike riding with Hunter, we talked, and I asked Jesus to be my Savior."

For about two seconds there was absolute silence, and then everyone started talking at once.

"Do you mean it?" asked Caleb.

"I knew it. I just knew it. I could tell that you have a new heart!" exclaimed Mary as she hugged her brother.

"God answered our prayers!" said Cassie.

Then Daniel, the charmer, walked over to Mac and shook his hand. "Welcome to the family, brother," he said in a very grown-up voice.

Everyone burst into laughter because that was exactly what Pastor Scotty said when someone joined the church—except he said "sister" if it was a woman.

Miss Jenny heard the excitement and arrived in the library just in time to hear the news. "Oh, Mac," she said as she threw her arms around him and almost smothered him with hugs. "Does Grace know?"

"I told her last night, but she kept it a secret so I could tell all of you today," he informed them.

"Well, I think we need to celebrate. You children listen to the story, and I'll get everyone to come over for shortbread." As she scurried to the kitchen, she called over her shoulder, "And we'll even have ice cream."

"My, my," remarked Sir John, "this is good news indeed. And our story today is about the good news of God's covenant to save His people from their sin."

"Is it another glory story?" asked Mary.

"Yes, it is, lassie." Sir John smiled. "And in this glory story we will discover another treasure of wisdom and knowledge."

The children got comfortable as Sir John continued, "When God made Adam and Eve, He made an agreement with them. He gave them one rule to obey. If they obeyed, they could continue to live in His presence in His garden."

"I know about that," declared Cassie. "They were not to eat from the Tree of the Knowledge of Good and Evil."

"Right you are, lassie," said Sir John. "Does anyone know what this agreement was called?"

After a few moments Caleb said, "You've stumped us, Sir John."

"It was called the 'covenant of works,'" explained Sir John. "Adam represented us in this covenant. He stood for the whole human race. So when he broke the covenant and disobeyed God, we all became sinners."

"And that's when the trouble started," Daniel pointed out.

"Yes, it is," said Sir John, "but it's also when God showed His wonderful grace. Adam and Eve were guilty, and they knew it. They knew they could no longer live in God's glorious presence because there can be no sin in God's presence. So they hid. God could have ended it all right there. Why do you suppose He didn't? Look up Ephesians 1:3-4."

"I know where Ephesians is," claimed Mac. "Hunter gave me this Bible yesterday, and he marked a verse in Ephesians." He opened his Bible and read: "'Blessed be the God and Father of our Lord Jesus Christ, who has blessed us in Christ with every spiritual blessing in the heavenly places, even as he chose us in him before the foundation of the world, that we should be holy and blameless before him.'"

"You see," continued Sir John, "Adam and Eve were no longer holy and blameless, but even before God created the world, the Father, Son, and Holy Spirit made a covenant to save their people from sin. This was not a covenant of works. This was a covenant of grace. Grace is God's love that we do not deserve and we cannot earn. Grace is a gift. Will someone read Ephesians 2:8-9?"

"That's the verse Hunter marked in my Bible," said Mac. Then he read: "'For by grace you have been saved through faith. And this is not your own doing; it is the gift of God, not a result of works, so that no one may boast.'"

Sir John explained, "Because of His grace, God did not leave Adam and Eve in their miserable condition. God *came* to the garden, and He *called* to Adam and Eve. He promised that one day He would send a Savior. Then God did something to show them that this Savior would die in their place and cover their sin with His righteousness so they could be holy and blameless again."

Cassie's eyes were wide with wonder. "I think I know what He did!" she exclaimed. "He killed the animal to make clothes for them."

"Ah, lassie, that is exactly right. God *came* to the garden, He *called* to Adam and Eve, and He *clothed* them. That is a picture of the covenant of grace. Jesus *comes* to us, and He *calls* us to be His children. He *clothes* us with His perfect righteousness. This is God's love that we cannot earn. It's a gift. It's grace."

"And it's the best gift in the whole world," added Mac.

Just then the doorbell rang, and soon the house was abuzz with excitement. Even Hunter, Pastor Scotty, Susie, and Angus came. Everyone crowded into the library, and Sir John announced, "Today we celebrate because God came into Mac's heart. He called Mac to be one of His children, and He clothed Mac with the righteousness of Jesus. He is a God of grace. Mac, please read Psalm 95:6-7, and you will discover a covenant value."

Hunter helped Mac find the verse in his Bible, and Mac read: "'Oh come, let us worship and bow down; let us kneel before the LORD, our Maker! For he is our God, and we are the people of his pasture, and the sheep of his hand.'"

The little group knelt down, and Hunter thanked God for His grace, and then Pastor Scotty asked the Lord to give Mac grace to live for His glory.

And then, of course, they had shortbread and ice cream.

LET'S TALK

Why had Caleb been jealous of Mac?

How did he get rid of his anger and jealousy?

What was Mac's announcement?

What was the covenant with Adam called?

When Adam and Eve sinned, what did God do?
(Clue—all the words begin with C.)

When did God choose us to belong to Him? (Ephesians 1:3-4)

What is this covenant called?

Since God is a God of grace, what should His people do?

Let's memorize God's Word: Psalm 95:6-7.

LET'S PRAY

Thank God for His wonderful grace and ask Him to help you to worship Him.

CHAPTER EIGHTEEN

The Pillow Fight

TREASURE OF WISDOM AND KNOWLEDGE: God is the God of grace.
COVENANT VALUE: Worship

Oh come, let us worship and bow down; let us kneel before the LORD, our Maker! For he is our God, and we are the people of his pasture, and the sheep of his hand. (Psalm 95:6-7)

———■———

"Okay, covenant kids, get your journals and tell us what you've been learning at Sir John's," instructed Dad as Cassie and Caleb gathered for family devotions. Caleb and his dad sat on the bed with pillows propped behind them. Cassie cuddled with her mother in the huge overstuffed rocking chair.

"We learned about the covenant of grace," said Caleb.

"Tell me some things you learned about the covenant of grace," requested their dad.

"Well," said Cassie, "when Adam sinned—"

"That's called the Fall," explained their dad.

"Oh, okay," continued Cassie. "After the Fall, God could have ended it all right there, but He didn't because He already had a plan—it's called the covenant of grace."

"Why is it called a covenant of grace?" asked their dad.

"Because they didn't deserve salvation, and they couldn't earn it. Grace is a gift," answered Caleb.

"Well," replied their dad, "you covenant kids really are learning a lot. Do you know when God made this covenant of grace?"

"Yes, sir," said Caleb. "Even before the world was made, God planned to save His people. So when Adam sinned, God *came* back to the garden—"

"And He *called* Adam," added Cassie.

"Wait a minute," said their mom. "I think I see a theme here. God *came* and He *called*—they both begin with C."

"Right, Mom," replied Caleb. "And then God did something else. Can you guess what it was?"

"Does it begin with C?" asked their mom.

Cassie and Caleb nodded.

"I think I know, but I don't think your dad knows," Mom teased.

"Wait a minute," protested their dad. "I think I know, but I don't think your mom knows."

"I think we have a little competition going here," laughed Caleb. "I have an idea—each of you write the answer."

"*Clever* kid," said their mom as she quickly wrote her answer and handed her paper to Cassie. Their dad folded his paper and gave it to Caleb.

"And what did my *charming* wife answer?" asked their dad.

"First let's hear from my *courageous* husband," their mom insisted.

"You two are the *corniest* parents," proclaimed Caleb.

"Enough! Stop with the C stuff," Cassie protested. "Drumroll please. Mom's answer is—*clothed*! Yeaaa, Mom! God *clothed* Adam and Eve with skins of animals, and He clothes us with the righteousness of Jesus."

Caleb opened his dad's paper with great fanfare and said, "And the big daddy's answer is . . . DAD! You just put a question mark! You let the girls win!"

Cassie and her mom gave each other a high five and started doing a victory dance. In fact they kept it up for quite a while. Finally they settled down. Caleb could hardly hide his grin. He looked pretty proud of himself when he said, "If you two *fallen females* are ready, we'll look at our journals."

"Ohhh," said their dad. "The Fall—*fallen females*. Now that's good. That's really good."

Suddenly a pillow flew across the room and hit Dad right in the face, and then it was all-out war. Everyone grabbed a pillow, and they had one gigantic pillow fight.

"Truce!" finally called their mom. "I'm exhausted! I think we need ice cream."

"Yeaa! Yes, we need ice cream," yelled Cassie.

They all filed into the kitchen. As they sat around the table eating ice cream with chocolate topping, their dad said, "Okay, let's try again, and this time we'll all be serious. So you learned about the covenant of grace. What is the treasure of wisdom and knowledge that you learned about God?"

"He's a God of grace," said Cassie. "And now we need to look up these verses to discover a covenant value."

Caleb looked up Psalm 29:2 and read: "'Ascribe to the LORD the glory due his name; worship the LORD in the splendor of holiness.'"

Cassie read Psalm 100:2 (NIV): "'Worship the LORD with gladness; come before him with joyful songs.'"

Their dad read Psalm 95:6-7: "'Oh come, let us worship and bow down; let us kneel before the LORD, our Maker! For he is our God, and we are the people of his pasture, and the sheep of his hand.'"

"I think I know the answer," declared Caleb. "I think it's worship."

"Right, Caleb," his dad responded. "And this is a very special covenant value because worship is the most important thing we do."

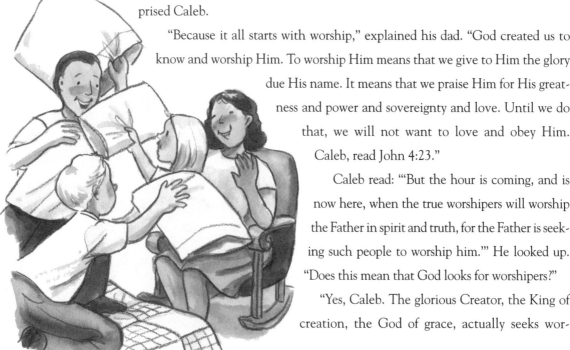

"The most important thing we do? Why is worship so important?" asked a surprised Caleb.

"Because it all starts with worship," explained his dad. "God created us to know and worship Him. To worship Him means that we give to Him the glory due His name. It means that we praise Him for His greatness and power and sovereignty and love. Until we do that, we will not want to love and obey Him. Caleb, read John 4:23."

Caleb read: "'But the hour is coming, and is now here, when the true worshipers will worship the Father in spirit and truth, for the Father is seeking such people to worship him.'" He looked up. "Does this mean that God looks for worshipers?"

"Yes, Caleb. The glorious Creator, the King of creation, the God of grace, actually seeks worshipers. He seeks people who will worship Him in spirit and in truth. That means He seeks people to worship in the power of the Holy Spirit and in the way He tells us to worship in His Word. I want to be one of those worshipers."

"Me too," said Cassie and Caleb together.

"Then we need to learn what God says about worship, and we need to pray for grace to worship Him in Spirit and in truth," said their dad. "We'll talk more about this tomorrow night, and we'll think about what it means to worship God."

LET'S TALK

Why is God's plan to save His people called a covenant of grace?

When did God make this plan?

When Adam and Eve sinned, what did God do?

What is the treasure of wisdom and knowledge in this story?

What is the covenant value?

What is the most important thing God's covenant children do?

Let's memorize God's Word: Psalm 95:6-7.

LET'S PRAY

Thank God for His wonderful grace and ask Him to help you to be a true worshiper.

CHAPTER NINETEEN

The Secret

**TREASURE OF WISDOM AND KNOWLEDGE: God is the God of grace.
COVENANT VALUE: Worship**

*Oh come, let us worship and bow down; let us kneel before the Lord, our Maker!
For he is our God, and we are the people of his pasture, and the sheep of his
hand. (Psalm 95:6-7)*

"Okay, kids, I have an assignment for you," said Dad as the family ate breakfast. "I have two Bible verses and a hymn that I want you to read several times today. We'll talk about them tonight during our devotion time. I put the assignment in your thinking places."

Cassie and Caleb each had a special *thinking place* where they liked to be alone and read and think. Cassie's *thinking place* was the big rocking chair in her parents' bedroom. To Cassie's mom this chair was one of her favorite places in the whole world. It had been in her room when she was a little girl, and she had sweet memories of sitting in this chair reading and thinking. Now it was one of Cassie's favorite places. She thought the chair even smelled good—like her mom's perfume.

Caleb's *thinking place* was his bed. He had several pillows to put behind his back, and he would sit there with all of his "treasures" within reach. There were shelves beside his bed with his drawing pad and pencils, his rock collection, his soccer trophies, and his books.

When they finished their chores, Cassie and Caleb hurried to their own special *thinking places*, but as soon as they looked at the assignment, they each hurried to the other's *thinking place*. They met halfway. In fact, they almost bumped into each other. "Do you think he knows?" asked Cassie.

"How could he? It's a secret. Mom doesn't even know. This is incredible," responded Caleb.

"What do you think we should do?" asked Cassie.

"Well, I think we should do the stuff Dad gave us to do and then go talk to Sir John," answered Caleb.

That is exactly what they did.

When they told Sir John about the assignment, he said, "Umm, I suppose you must make a decision. Should you tell your dad the secret, or should you wait until next week? But if you decide to tell him, then you will need to work all day to be ready."

The children thought for a few minutes. Then Caleb spoke. "I think the time is right. I think we should tell him tonight."

"I agree," squealed Cassie in excitement.

"But do you think you can be ready?" asked Sir John.

"We're almost ready now," answered Caleb. "It'll just take a little more practice."

"Then let's get started," urged Sir John.

After dinner Caleb turned to his father. "Dad, may we have devotion time in the den?"

"Sure. Maybe then we won't be tempted to have a pillow fight." He grinned. "Did you do the assignment?"

"Yes, sir!" said Cassie and Caleb together.

"Good. Last night we talked about worship. To worship God means to give Him the glory due His name. It means that we acknowledge His greatness and power and sovereignty and love. We can worship God because we were cre-ated in His image and because He has saved us by His grace. Worship is the most important thing we do. Caleb, will you read the first verse on your assignment?"

Caleb read Romans 12:1: "'I appeal to you there-fore, brothers, by the mercies of God, to present your bodies as a living sacrifice, holy and acceptable to God, which is your spiritual worship.'" Caleb had a puzzled look on his face. "Dad, I've been thinking about this, but I'm not sure what it means."

"Well, Caleb, God is teaching us that worship is not just something we do when we go to church on

Sunday. For the Christian, our whole life is to be an act of worship. We are to do everything for God's glory. Whether we are working or playing, we are to remember that we belong to God, and we are to live for His glory. Cassie, read the second verse on your assignment."

Cassie read Hebrews 12:28: "'Therefore let us be grateful for receiving a kingdom that cannot be shaken, and thus let us offer to God acceptable worship, with reverence and awe.'"

"Kids," continued Dad, "one of the things I want you to learn from this verse is that when we gather with God's people to worship Him, we are to worship in a way that is acceptable to Him. We are to worship Him the way He tells us to worship in His Word. We are to worship Him in Spirit and in truth. We are also to worship Him with reverence and awe because He is a holy and majestic God. We should not be lazy when we worship. We should pay close attention to everything in the worship service, and we should ask God to help us to please Him in the way we worship. Now did you read the hymn?"

Cassie and Caleb had been waiting for this moment. "Dad, we know that this is your favorite hymn, and we have an early birthday present for you," announced Caleb. "We had planned to give it to you next week, but we think we should give it to you tonight."

Cassie went to the piano, Caleb got his trumpet, and they played a duet of "O Worship the King." Then they sang the three verses that Sir John had helped them memorize.

Cassie and Caleb's parents were speechless. Finally their dad said, "That is the best gift you have ever given me, and I'm glad you gave it to me tonight."

LET'S TALK

What was the assignment that Cassie and Caleb's dad gave them?

What was the secret?

Where were Cassie and Caleb's thinking places?

Do you have a favorite thinking place?

What do we learn about worship from Romans 12:1?

What do we learn about worship from Hebrews 12:28?

Let's memorize God's Word: Psalm 95:6-7.

LET'S PRAY

Thank God for His wonderful grace, and ask Him to help you to worship Him with reverence and awe.

O Worship the King

1. O worship the King all - glo - rious a - bove, O grate - ful - ly
2. O tell of his might, O sing of his grace, whose robe is the
3. The earth with its store of won - ders un - told, Al - might - y, your
4. Your boun - ti - ful care what tongue can re - cite? It breathes in the

sing his pow'r and his love; our shield and De - fend - er, the
light, whose can - o - py space. His char - iots of wrath the deep
pow'r has found - ed of old; has 'stab - lished it fast by a
air; it shines in the light; it streams from the hills; it de -

An - cient of Days, pa - vil - ioned in splen - dor and gird - ed with praise.
thun - der - clouds form, and dark is his path on the wings of the storm.
change - less de - cree, and round it has cast, like a man - tle, the sea.
scends to the plain; and sweet - ly dis - tils in the dew and the rain.

5. Frail children of dust, and feeble as frail,
   in you do we trust, nor find you to fail;
   your mercies how tender, how firm to the end,
   our Maker, Defender, Redeemer, and Friend!

6. O measureless Might! Ineffable Love!
   While angels delight to hymn you above,
   the humbler creation, though feeble their lays,
   with true adoration shall lisp to your praise.

CHAPTER TWENTY

The Sunday Disaster

TREASURE OF WISDOM AND KNOWLEDGE: God is the God of grace.

COVENANT VALUE: Worship

Oh come, let us worship and bow down; let us kneel before the LORD, our Maker! For he is our God, and we are the people of his pasture, and the sheep of his hand. (Psalm 95:6-7)

Everyone was quiet as they drove out of the church parking lot. The silence was terrible, but Cassie and Caleb knew it would be even worse when their mom and dad did start talking. Finally their dad said, "I admit that I would like to just punish you two and forget the whole thing, but I know that I have to assume part of the responsibility for what happened. So I think we all need to think and pray, and then we'll talk about this later today."

After lunch Cassie and Caleb went to their rooms for their Sunday afternoon rest and read time. They love to read, but they both had trouble concentrating today. They kept thinking about what had happened during the worship service and dreading what their parents would do. Finally the moment came. Their dad called, "Okay, kids, come to our room, and we'll talk."

Their mom and dad were sitting on the bed, and Cassie and Caleb sat in the big rocker. Somehow it seemed safer to be together.

"Your mom and I have been talking and praying," began their dad. "We want to be sure you both understand what happened today because it's not just that you caused a real commotion during the worship service. We're afraid that you have a heart problem."

"A heart problem!" gasped Caleb. "What's wrong with my heart?"

"Am I going to have a heart attack?" shrieked Cassie.

Their parents laughed and shook their heads. "You kids do have a way of redirecting the conversation," said their mom.

"We're not talking about your heart that pumps blood," explained their dad. "We're talking about your spiritual hearts. We're talking about that part of us that worships God in Spirit and in truth."

"Oooh," said Caleb. "The part that worships with reverence and awe."

"Exactly," said their dad. "All week we have been talking about worship being a covenant value for God's people. We have even said that worship is the most important thing we do. But after today your mom and I realized that we have not done our part to show you how to prepare your hearts for worship. We're not going to punish you . . ."

A huge sigh of relief came from the big rocker.

". . . but we do want to talk about what we can all do so that nothing like this happens again," continued their dad. "So let's start at the beginning. When do you think the problem started?"

"Well," began Caleb, "everything was real quiet since Pastor Scotty had just finished praying. The only sound was Mr. Curly-Pepper snoring."

"Really loud," added Cassie. (When Cassie first learned to talk, she thought Mr. Rufus Culpepper's name was Curly-Pepper, and somehow the name stuck. Now everyone lovingly called him Mr. Curly-Pepper.)

Caleb continued, "And it was funny, and Angus and I were trying not to laugh, but then I dropped my hymn book!"

"Then," said Cassie trying not to laugh, "Mr. Curly-Pepper jumped because of the loud bang when the book hit the floor."

"Yeah, and talk about a heart problem! He almost had a heart attack," finished Caleb.

"And then Susie and I got so tickled we lost control, and mom had to take us out," added Cassie.

Cassie noticed that her mom had her hand over her face. Cassie felt terrible because she thought her mom was crying. Then she realized that Mom was trying to hide laughter. Cassie and Caleb could hardly believe it when their mom finally burst out laughing and then said apologetically, "Okay, okay—I can't help it! Sweet Mr. Curly-Pepper goes to sleep and snores every Sunday. Since he sits right in front of me, I see him nodding. What happened today really was funny!"

Their dad shook his head, and Cassie and Caleb were sure that he was trying not to laugh. "Actually," he said, "that's not when the trouble began. It all started on Saturday. We did not prepare our hearts to worship the Lord. Then the trouble got worse when we agreed to let you have friends sit with you. Children need to sit with their own parents during worship so they can experience worship together as a family and so they won't be tempted to be distracted. When I saw you writing notes on the bulletin and whispering during the hymns, I knew we had made a mistake."

"And it all went downhill from there," declared Caleb.

Their dad agreed. "I admit that what happened was funny, and it'll make a good story for you to tell your children someday—"

"But my kids had better not *ever* do anything like that!" interrupted Cassie before she thought about what she was saying.

"And I don't want my kids to ever do anything like that again," replied her dad. "So this is what we're going to do. Every Monday Pastor Scotty is going to put the hymns for Sunday on the church website. We'll talk about those hymns during the week. On Saturday during our devotion time, we'll talk about what it means to worship the Lord, and we'll pray that He will prepare our hearts for worship. On Sunday morning as we ride to church, Mom will read some Psalms to us, and we'll sing 'O Worship the King.' That way our hearts will be more prepared. And our family rule is that you will always sit with us, and you don't invite your friends to sit with you. On the way home from church, we all will share one thing we heard in the sermon."

"That sounds like a good plan, Dad," said Caleb, the organized one.

"Well, to tell you the truth, I didn't think of it all by myself. I've been talking with Susie and Angus's dad, and we decided on this together. And your mom had a great idea. She invited them over for ice cream sundaes."

"Yikes!" exclaimed Cassie. "You mean we have to face Pastor Scotty. I know he must be really mad at Angus and Susie and at us."

Just then the doorbell rang. Caleb answered the door. "Hello," he said sheepishly.

"Hi, kids!" exclaimed Pastor Scotty, as cheerful as ever.

Cassie and Caleb looked at each other and then back at Pastor Scotty.

"Uh-h," Cassie stuttered, "you're not upset with us?"

"No, kids," said Pastor Scotty. "I talked with your parents, and we're going to be thinking about how we can help all the kids at church understand what's going on in the worship service. And you know, another good thing came from this."

"What?" exclaimed the kids together.

"Well," chuckled Pastor Scotty, "I'll bet Mr. Curly-Pepper won't be sleeping during my sermons anymore!"

LET'S TALK

What happened during the worship service?

What are some of the things that caused the trouble?

What is Cassie and Caleb's family going to do now to prepare for worship?

What could your family do to prepare for worship?

Let's memorize God's Word: Psalm 95:6-7.

LET'S PRAY

Ask God to prepare your heart to worship Him with reverence and awe.

CHAPTER TWENTY-ONE

Glory Story—
God Makes a Promise

GENESIS 12

TREASURE OF WISDOM AND KNOWLEDGE: God is a covenant keeper.

COVENANT VALUE: Obedience

[Jesus said] "If you love me, you will obey what I command." (John 14:15 NIV)

———■———

"Hello, children," said Miss Jenny. Her welcoming hugs, the smell of shortbread, the sight of Sir John's "For Christ's Crown and Covenant" banner, and the warm smile of the dignified old Scottish gentleman had become quite familiar to the children, but going to their house still seemed like a grand adventure.

"Do we get to hear another glory story today?" asked Cassie as she walked into Sir John's library and settled onto the soft leather couch.

"Ah, yes, lassie. Today we will hear how God made a glorious promise to Abraham," replied Sir John.

"Who was Abraham?" asked Mary.

"Good question, lassie. Turn in your Bibles to Genesis 12. Caleb, read verses 1-3."

Caleb read: "'Now the Lord said to Abram, "Go from your country and your kindred and your father's house to the land that I will show you. And I will make of you a great nation, and I will bless you and make your name great, so that you will be a blessing. I will bless those who bless you, and him who dishonors you I will curse, and in you all the families of the earth shall be blessed."'"

Sir John continued, "God *came* to Abraham and *called* him to leave His own country and go to the land God promised to give him."

"Wait a minute!" cried Caleb. "God *came* to Abraham and *called* him—that's just what God did to Adam! Don't you remember? God *came*, and He *called*."

"Splendid!" said Sir John. "You're beginning to see the connections."

"What do you mean?" asked Caleb. "What connections?"

"Let me explain," began Sir John. "All of the Bible is connected. From the beginning God shows us Himself and His promise to send a Savior. If we just look at one part of the Bible, and we don't know how it is connected to the rest of the Bible, we don't really understand that part. Let me see if I can think of an example." Sir John scratched his head. "I've got it! Wait just a minute, children." He left the room and soon returned with Miss Jenny and a bundle and a basket. "What do you see in this basket?" he asked.

"Little pieces of cloth," answered Cassie.

"Each of you take one piece of cloth and tell me about it," instructed Sir John.

Each child described the piece chosen, and then Sir John said, "You told me something about the color and shape and texture of your piece of cloth, but you didn't tell me about its purpose because you didn't see it connected to the other pieces." He nodded to Miss Jenny, who unfolded the bundle. It was one of her handmade quilts.

"Oooh," gasped Mary. "It's beautiful!"

"You see, children," explained Sir John, "if you just look at each piece of cloth, and you don't see it connected to all the other pieces, you miss the beauty and even the real meaning of the individual pieces. The more we understand God's Word, the more we will see how all the parts are connected to show us what God is like and to tell us about His promise to save His people. It's wonderful that you're beginning to see the connections. Now let's continue. God came to Abraham and told him about the covenant promise. God promised to be Abraham's God. He promised to give Abraham so many children that they would become a great nation."

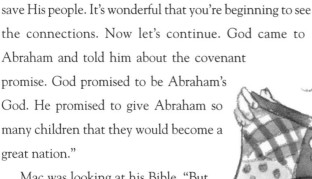

Mac was looking at his Bible. "But how would all people be blessed through Abraham?" he asked.

Sir John's eyes twinkled. "Ah, lad, what a good detective you are. You're looking closely at the verses, and that's how you'll discover the treasures. Think back to the garden. God promised Adam and Eve that He would send a Savior. Then God told Abraham that this Savior would come from his family. People all over the world and all through history are blessed because Jesus came to die for our sin."

Mary exclaimed, "So Jesus came from Abraham's family! I wish I were part of Abraham's family."

Sir John smiled. "Well, lassie, I have another wonderful connection for you. Turn to Galatians 3:29."

The children quickly turned the pages in their Bibles. "I've got it," called Daniel. He read: "'And if you are Christ's, then you are Abraham's offspring, heirs according to promise.'"

Sir John explained, "All Christians who have ever lived anywhere on this planet and all those who will come after us are the spiritual children of Abraham. So, Mary, you *are* part of Abraham's family. Now I have a question for you. Why do you think God chose Abraham to be the father of His covenant family?"

"Uhmm," replied Mac, "Abraham must have been a really, really good man."

"Actually, Mac," continued Sir John, "there was nothing special about Abraham. He was not a worshiper of God. He was not looking for God. He was not thinking about God. He did not even believe in God. But God chose Abraham and gave him a new heart so that he could believe the promise."

"Just like He did for us!" declared Daniel. "This makes me think about Jeremiah 24:7. He began reciting the verse, and all the children joined in: "'I will give them a heart to know that I am the LORD, and they shall be my people and I will be their God, for they shall return to me with their whole heart.'"

"Splendid, splendid, splendid!" exclaimed Sir John. "Connections, connections, connections. What fine Bible scholars you are. Now when God made this promise, there was a slight problem. Actually it was a HUGE problem. Abraham and his wife, Sarah, did not have children, and they were too old to have any. How could God possibly keep His promise to give Abraham a family so big it would become a great nation? Abraham had no idea *how*, but he believed God *could* and *would* keep the promise. Cassie, read Genesis 12:4 to discover what Abraham did."

Cassie read: "'So Abram went, as the LORD had told him—'"

"Amazing," interrupted Mac. "Abraham just left. He did what God told him. He sure was an obedient dude."

Sir John laughed. "Yes, Mac, Abraham was obedient. But let's think about *why* Abraham obeyed. It was because God came to him and called him. God made Himself known to Abraham and gave Abraham a heart to know Him. Abraham's obedience is a beautiful part of this story, but the most glorious part is that the God of grace and glory came to Abraham and made a promise. And God kept the promise when Jesus came into this world."

All the children nodded in agreement.

Sir John continued, "So our treasure of wisdom and knowledge is that God is a covenant keeper. You'll have to look up the clues in your journal to discover the covenant value."

"Uhmm," said Daniel, "I won't be surprised if the covenant value is obedience. So just give me the word that it's time for us to go to the kitchen for shortbread, and I'll obey."

LET'S TALK

What did God promise Abraham?

Why did this story remind Caleb of Adam?

What did Sir John mean by connections?

Who is part of Abraham's family?

Why did God choose Abraham to be the father of His covenant family? (Deuteronomy 7:6-8.)

Why did Abraham obey God?

What treasure of wisdom and knowledge did you learn about God in this story?

Let's memorize God's Word: John 14:15.

LET'S PRAY

Thank God that He kept His promise and sent Jesus to be our Savior.

CHAPTER TWENTY-TWO

Bicycle Rack for Three

TREASURE OF WISDOM AND KNOWLEDGE: God is a covenant keeper.

COVENANT VALUE: Obedience

[Jesus said] "If you love me, you will obey what I command." (John 14:15 NIV)

———■———

"Yep." Mac nodded. "It's obedience all right. Every one of these verses talks about obedience." Mac and Caleb were on the front porch looking up the clues in their journals.

"You're right," agreed Caleb as he read the verses:

"'Give me understanding, and I will keep your law and obey it with all my heart. (Psalm 119:34 NIV)'

"'I have kept my feet from every evil path so that I might obey your word. (Psalm 119:101 NIV)'

"'If you love me, you will obey what I command. (John 14:15 NIV)'

"'We know that we have come to know him if we obey his commands. (1 John 2:3 NIV)'"

"No doubt about it. The covenant value is obedience," Mac said as he closed his journal.

"So what do you want to do today?" asked Caleb.

"Well," started Mac. "Uhh . . ."

Caleb looked at Mac. He knew his friend was stalling. "What?" asked Caleb. "What's wrong?"

"You see, I'm kinda . . ." Mac stopped mid-sentence and turned to look as a car pulled into the driveway. It took Caleb about half a second to figure out that Mac was going mountain bike riding with Hunter.

"Hey, guys," called Hunter as he hopped out of his car, "guess what?"

"What?" they quickly answered.

"I got a new mount for my bike roof rack, and now I can carry three bikes on my car! Do you want to go with us, Caleb?"

Caleb had never moved so fast. He ran into the house, got permission from his mom, ran into the garage, grabbed his bike and helmet, and was back before Hunter had loaded Mac's bike on the roof rack.

By the time they got to the bike trails, Caleb's face was starting to hurt from smiling so much. As they unloaded the bikes, Hunter said, "Tell me about your visit with Sir John this week."

"This week our treasure of wisdom and knowledge is that God is a covenant keeper, and our covenant value is obedience," replied Mac.

"Good value," said Hunter. "Okay, let's ride, and then we'll talk."

Off they went. Caleb was so excited he still couldn't stop grinning. They rode through the parking area and down a gravel road. Soon the road turned to dirt and then just seemed to end. "This is where it gets fun, guys!" Hunter called as he dove down a small trail just wide enough for one bike at a time. "See if you can keep up!"

The trail was difficult, with branches sticking out and big roots in the ground. Caleb was glad he was wearing his helmet. They flew down a steep hill, through a creek, and then down the *curviest* trail the boys had ever been on. Finally the trail widened again, and Hunter slowed down. "That's called 'single-track', and it's my favorite," he told them.

Caleb and Mac could both feel their hearts pounding. "I . . . like . . . single . . . track . . . too," Mac managed between gasps for air.

"I think we need a break," Hunter laughed. The boys got their water bottles and stretched out on the grass. "So what have you learned about obedience?" Hunter quizzed.

Mac started. "I've learned that God loves it when we obey Him, and the more we obey Him, the more He loves us."

"Hmm . . . did Sir John tell you that?" Hunter asked.

"No." Mac shook his head. "I figured that out on my own."

"I thought so," said Hunter. "Let me help you get this straight. God loves us completely. We cannot earn His love. When we belong to Him, He sees us covered with the righteousness of Jesus. He loves us like He loves Jesus. We can't do anything to make Him love us more or to make Him love us less."

"Really?" exclaimed Mac. "Then why should we obey Him at all if He's going to love us anyway?"

Caleb spoke up. "I think I know. It's like the verse in our journal. We obey Him because *we love Him.*"

"Exactly," Hunter responded. "You see, boys, the more we get to know God and the more we understand how much He loves us, the more we'll love Him back, and the more we'll want to show our love by obeying Him."

Mac thought about this and then said, "You know, I'm starting to learn more about God, and you're right. I want to do things that please Him, and I guess it's because I'm loving Him more."

Hunter smiled. "Caleb and Mac, I want to be sure you understand about obedience. God knows how weak we are. He has not left us alone to figure out what we are to do or to have the power to do it. God has given us His Word and His Holy Spirit. His Word gives us the directions, and His Spirit gives us the power. . . . Okay, let's ride some more."

Caleb and Mac jumped on their bikes and followed Hunter. Soon there was a fork in the trail, and Hunter stopped to wait for them.

"Which way do we go?" asked Caleb.

"I wanna go *that* way." Mac pointed. "Look at that steep hill! That looks fun."

"That's why I stopped and waited for you two," Hunter explained. "That way is dangerous, and I don't want you to go on that path."

"Hey," said Mac, "that's like that verse we read—you know, the one about the evil path."

"I know the one you're talking about." Caleb nodded. "It's Psalm 119:101: 'I have kept my feet from every evil path so that I might obey your word.'"

"Well, guys," Hunter informed them, "I'm keeping you from *that* evil path so you can finish this ride, and I hope this will help you to remember to stay away from evil paths that will lead you to sin."

As they rode off, Caleb was still grinning. It had been the greatest day. "Come on, guys!" Hunter called. "See if you can catch me. And, Caleb, you had better close your mouth, or you're going to catch some bugs!"

■

LET'S TALK

What is the treasure of wisdom and knowledge in this story?

What is the covenant value?

Does God love us more if we obey Him?

Why should we obey God?

Where has God given us the directions so that we know how to obey Him?

Who has God given so that we will have the power to obey?

Let's memorize God's Word: John 14:15.

■

LET'S PRAY

Ask God to help you to love Him more.
Ask Him to help you show your love by obeying His Word.

CHAPTER TWENTY-THREE

Trust and Obey

TREASURE OF WISDOM AND KNOWLEDGE: God is a covenant keeper.
COVENANT VALUE: Obedience

[Jesus said] "If you love me, you will obey what I command." (John 14:15 NIV)

———■———

All week the very same thing was happening in several homes. Many parents had looked on the church web page to find out what the hymns would be for the following Sunday, and families had been singing them. When the children gathered at Sir John's house, Cassie said, "Sir John, this is so cool. Our covenant value for this week is obedience, and one of the hymns we'll sing Sunday morning is 'Trust and Obey.'"

The children knew what the old gentleman would say, and as soon as he started speaking, they joined with him, "Splendid, splendid, splendid!"

Sir John laughed and then said, "I have a wonderful idea. Before we talk about our covenant value, let's sing 'Trust and Obey.'"

"Will you play your bagpipe?" asked Cassie.

"But of course, lassie," replied Sir John.

The bagpipe and the children's voices made a glorious sound. Then Sir John told the children to open their journals. "Today I want us to talk about all of the treasures we have discovered and the covenant values we have learned. First we learned that God is our glorious Creator. What should this knowledge about God make us want to do?"

"Reflect His glory!" exclaimed Caleb.

Sir John continued, "And since God is King of creation, what should His covenant people do?"

"I know," grinned Daniel. "We should get into Stewart's ship and be good stewards of everything God gives us."

Sir John laughed. "And since God is the God of grace, what should we do?"

"We should worship Him," answered Cassie.

"Splendid, splendid, splendid," said an excited Sir John. "Oh, my young scholars, you're solving the mystery. You're discovering treasures. The more we know about God, the more we will become like Him. When we understand that all of the Bible tells us about Jesus, we will be transformed by the power of the Gospel. Oh, the wonder of the mystery of the Gospel!"

The children didn't exactly understand all that Sir John said, but they knew that he had discovered wonderful treasures, and they wanted to find more of these riches.

On Sunday many children arrived at church with a new sense of purpose. They had been singing "Trust and Obey" all week, and they were excited about the worship service. During Sunday school their teacher said, "Kids, we have a surprise for you today. Our elders want to help you to be prepared to participate in the worship service so that you can worship God with reverence and awe. So Pastor Scotty is going to come and give us a preview of the sermon."

When Pastor Scotty arrived, he gave the children a kids' bulletin. He told them that he would be preaching from Luke 24:13-35 and asked them to find this passage in their Bibles and to mark it with the bulletin. He explained that when it was time to read the Scripture, he wanted them to follow along in their own Bibles.

Susie raised her hand. "Dad, why do we always stand when you read the Bible in church?"

"Good question, Susie," responded Pastor Scotty. "The Bible is not just another book. This is the very Word of God. We stand to show our reverence for God's Word." Then Pastor Scotty showed the children some questions on their bulletins. "During the sermon I want you to listen carefully and see if you hear the answers to these questions," he explained.

During the worship service everyone could tell that the children were not so wiggly. They stood and sang the hymns. They didn't draw on their bulletins. And there seemed to be a holy hush when they stood while Pastor Scotty read the Scripture. Then when he began preaching, the children listened intently to try and hear the answers to the questions in their bulletins. Pastor Scotty thought that the adults listened better too.

In his sermon the pastor said that after the Resurrection, two of the disciples were walking together. As he preached, you could see all of the children writing on their bulletins, but they weren't writing notes to each other. They were answering the questions.

"Where were the disciples going (Luke 24:13)?" *Answer: To Emmaus.*

"Who joined them (v. 15)?" *Answer: Jesus.*

"Did the disciples recognize Jesus (v. 16)?" *Answer: No.*

"Why were the disciples sad (v. 19-20)?" *Answer: Because Jesus had been put to death.*

"What kind of hearts did Jesus say they had (v. 25)?" *Answer: Slow to believe.*

"What did Jesus do (v. 27)?" *Answer: He explained what was said in the Scriptures about Himself.*

"Where in the Scriptures did He begin (v. 27)?" *Answer: With Moses and the prophets.*

Pastor Scotty explained, "Jesus showed them Old Testament verses that told about Himself. He showed them that all of the Bible tells us about God's promise to send a Savior, and He is that Savior."

Cassie, Caleb, Daniel, Mary, and Mac were thinking, *Connections, connections, connections.*

Sir John was thinking, *I hope my young friends are seeing the connections.*

Pastor Scotty continued preaching, and the children continued answering questions.

"What happened to the disciples' hearts when they understood that all of the Bible tells us about Jesus (v. 32)?" "Answer: Their hearts burned."

Pastor Scotty explained, "This does not mean that they had heartburn! It means their hearts were full of warm love for Jesus." Then he asked the next question. "What did the disciples do (v. 33)?" "Answer: They returned to Jerusalem."

"What did they tell the other disciples (v. 34)?" "Answer: It was true that the Lord had risen!"

Pastor Scotty explained, "When we see Jesus on every page of Scripture, then we understand what the Bible is all about. When we see Him—not with our physical eyes but with our spiritual eyes—we know that we can trust Him, and our hearts will be full of love for Him. This love will cause us to want to go and tell others that He is alive. This love will cause us to want to obey Him."

The final hymn was "Trust and Obey," and everyone sang it with great gusto!

LET'S TALK

Since God is the glorious Creator, what should we do?

Since God is the King of creation, name something we should do.

Since God is the God of grace, what should we do?

Since God is a covenant keeper, what should we do?

What are some of the things Pastor Scotty did to help the children worship with reverence and awe?

What did you learn from the questions in the kids' bulletin?

Let's memorize God's Word: John 14:15.

LET'S PRAY

Ask God to help you to love Him more. Ask Him to help you trust and obey Him.

Trust and Obey

CHAPTER TWENTY-FOUR

The Mountain Bike Race

TREASURE OF WISDOM AND KNOWLEDGE: God is a covenant keeper.
COVENANT VALUE: Obedience

[Jesus said] "If you love me, you will obey what I command." (John 14:15 NIV)

———■———

"Here he comes!" cried Mac. Caleb and Mac had been bike riding with Hunter every Saturday for several weeks, and they were both getting pretty good.

"Hey, guys," Hunter called even before he got out of his car, "have I got news for you!"

"What?" Caleb and Mac asked expectantly.

Hunter jumped out of his car and started loading the bikes. "Every year there's an event called the State Games. They have all kinds of competitions like volleyball, running races, and archery. I entered the mountain bike race."

"Wowwwee!" the boys exclaimed. "Can we go and watch?"

"Watch! I've got bigger plans for you guys. This year there's a new bike race category for *your* age group!"

Caleb and Mac were speechless. Finally Mac said slowly, "Do you mean . . ."

"Yep!" said Hunter. "I've already talked to your parents, and they said it will be fine for you to enter the race. But this means we'll have to go riding more often because you've got to be ready."

"You mean like . . . *train?*" asked Mac.

Hunter laughed. "Absolutely! From now on you boys are in training."

"Cool," proclaimed Caleb.

When Mac and Caleb told Sir John about the race, he smiled. "Ah, lads, have I got a story for you. Have you ever heard about the great Scottish runner Eric Liddell?"

The boys shook their heads.

"Eric was a fine Christian. He lived for God's glory, and he ran for God's glory. He once said, 'When I run, I feel God's pleasure.' He was chosen to be on the Olympic team, but when he arrived at the big games, the race he was supposed to run was scheduled for Sunday. Eric said that he could not run on the Sabbath. Everyone tried to persuade him, but he would not disobey God. So on Sunday Eric went to church, and someone else ran the race."

"He didn't get to run?" asked Mac.

"Not in the race he had trained for," explained Sir John. "But he ran in another race on another day."

"Did he win?" asked both boys together.

"Yes, lads, he did. But more important than that, Eric obeyed God. Whether you eat or drink, or ride in a race, always remember to do it for God's glory. Then you will know His pleasure," urged Sir John.

Finally the big day came. The racers had to arrive early to register, and so Hunter picked up Mac and Caleb. Everyone was there to see them off. Cassie and Mary had signs that said, "Go, Mac!" and "Go, Caleb!" While they were loading the bikes, Sir John and Miss Jenny came hurrying down the street—well, they were hurrying as fast as Sir John can hurry. He was carrying a sign with the words "For Christ's Crown and Covenant."

"Don't forget, lads," he said, "ride for God's glory, and you will feel His pleasure."

"We'll be there to see you race!" everyone called out as the three pulled out of the driveway.

"I am sooo excited!" Mac exclaimed as they drove to the mountain bike trail.

"I'm really proud of you guys," said Hunter. "You've trained hard for this, and I hope you both have a great time."

They arrived at the race site and found a

rather large crowd. "Wow," said Caleb. "I didn't know there would be so many people." They followed Hunter to the registration table. Soon they were registered and numbered. Caleb kept looking at the number pinned to his bike. He decided he would never take that number off. He was a real racer now, and nothing could ruin this day.

"Okay, let's go look at the course and practice," said Hunter. "The course is a two-mile loop. My category will go around it ten times, but your category will just make one lap." Caleb and Mac were relieved to hear that. "You guys ride around and warm up. I'll be back to get you later. I've got to warm up for my race."

Mac and Caleb were awed by the size of the crowd. They were riding around slowly, looking over the course, when a bigger boy flew up behind them and ran right into Caleb. "What're you doing in my way!" he demanded. "You're just a little squirt. You're not old enough to be here."

Caleb could feel all the blood rushing to his head. He could feel his fists clenching. Then suddenly lots of things ran through his mind at once. He remembered John 14:15 (NIV): "If you love me, you will obey what I command." He remembered his Sunday school lesson from 1 Peter 3:9 (NIV): "Do not repay evil with evil or insult with insult, but with blessing, because to this you were called." He remembered Sir John's story about Eric Liddell. He prayed silently, *Lord, please help me to glorify You. Please give me the strength to obey You.*

Caleb's fists relaxed, and his head started feeling normal. He was surprised at how calm his voice sounded. "I'm sorry I was in your way. Hope you have a good race today."

"Uhh . . . yeah," said the boy with a puzzled look on his face. He got back on his bike and rode off just as Hunter arrived on the scene.

"What was that all about?" he asked.

"Caleb was so great!" said Mac, and then he told Hunter the whole story.

"It wasn't me," declared Caleb. "I wanted to hit him, but I prayed, and God helped me. It's like He put the words in my mouth."

Hunter gave Caleb a high five. "Caleb," he said, "as far as I'm concerned, you've already won the race."

"Yeah!" said Mac. "I feel God's pleasure on *you.*"

About that time a voice came over the loudspeaker: "All beginners age twelve and under report to the starting line."

Caleb and Mac had a great time racing around the course. Did they win? Not exactly. Caleb came in thirty-first place, and Mac came in twenty-ninth, but they had so much fun they didn't care.

"We'll get 'em next year," panted Mac as they crossed the finish line.

---■---

LET'S TALK

Why didn't Eric Liddell, the Scottish Olympic runner, run in his race?

What did he say he felt when he ran?

What happened to Caleb while he was warming up for the race?

What did he want to do?

What did he remember?

Who do you think reminded him of these things?

What did he do?

Let's memorize God's Word: John 14:15.

---■---

LET'S PRAY

Ask God to give you wisdom and strength to obey Him even when it is hard.

CHAPTER TWENTY-FIVE

Glory Story— The Smoking Firepot

GENESIS 15

TREASURE OF WISDOM AND KNOWLEDGE: God is our shield and reward.

COVENANT VALUE: Trust

Trust in the LORD with all your heart, and do not lean on your own understanding. In all your ways acknowledge him, and he will make straight your paths. (Proverbs 3:5-6)

"Hi, Angus," called Mary and Mac as they met Daniel, Cassie, and Caleb to walk to Sir John's house. Angus had spent the night with Caleb and was going with them.

As they walked, Daniel spoke. "You know, Angus, when Caleb first told us about our summer adventure, I thought it was a bad joke. But going to Sir John's has been really fun."

"Yeah," said Cassie. "We've discovered some great treasures."

"Especially us," said Mary. "Mac and I discovered the greatest treasure of all."

Mac nodded in agreement. "It's still hard for me to believe that I belong to Jesus and that He will *never* leave me."

The children were quiet. They all knew that Mac was thinking about how his own dad had left him.

"Welcome, Angus," said Sir John. "We're glad you've joined us today. So what have you lads and lassies been discussing on your walk here?"

Daniel spoke for the group. "We were all telling Angus that we love coming to see you and Miss Jenny every week."

Cassie added, "Mary said she and Mac have discovered the greatest treasure of all. And Mac said it's still hard for him to believe that he belongs to Jesus and that Jesus will never leave him."

Sir John seemed to understand. "Well, my fine scholars," he said, "I think your conversation leads right into our story for today."

"Is it another glory story?" asked Mary.

"Ah, lassie, we'll see. Children, Mac said the very thing that all of us think sometimes. It's hard to understand that we belong to God and that He will never leave us. Abraham wondered about this same thing. God had promised to make Abraham's family so big that they would become a great nation. But what was the problem?"

"Abraham didn't have any children," answered Cassie.

"Exactly, lassie," said Sir John. "Many years passed. Abraham and Sarah still had no children. Abraham was almost a hundred years old. Would God really keep His promise? Daniel, read Genesis 15:1."

Daniel read: "'After these things the word of the Lord came to Abram in a vision: "Fear not, Abram, I am your shield; your reward shall be very great."'"

Sir John continued, "I am sure Abraham was thrilled that God was his shield and that his reward would be very great. But Abraham still wondered how God was going to keep the promise to give him lots of children. Mary, read verse 5 to discover what God told Abraham."

Mary read: "'And he [God] brought him outside and said, "Look toward heaven, and number the stars, if you are able to number them." Then he said to him, "So shall your offspring be."'"

Mac gasped, "Do you mean Abraham and Sarah had as many children as there are stars in the sky?"

Sir John smiled. "Think, lad, think. What did we learn in Galatians 3:29?"

"Oh yeah," replied Mac. "If we belong to Christ, then we are part of Abraham's family. Well, I guess if you think about all the Christians all over the world and all the Christians who have ever lived, that would be so many that we couldn't count them."

"Yes, indeed," said Sir John. "But God can count them. And He knows every one of us by name. Abraham believed God, but he asked God a question. Mac, read verse 8."

Mac read: "'But he said, "O Lord GOD, how am I to know that I shall possess it?"'"

Sir John explained, "Abraham believed, but he was like you, Mac. The promise was so wonderful that it was almost more than he could believe. It's like he was saying, 'O sovereign Lord, I believe—but how can I *know*? How can I *really know* that You will keep Your promise?' Then God did an incredible thing to tell Abraham, and us, that we can be absolutely sure that He will keep His promise to be our God and to be with us always. This is what happened."

Sir John's voice was full of wonder as he continued. "The Lord told Abraham to bring some animals, to kill them and cut them in half, and to line them up opposite each other so that there was a path between them. The sun began to set, Abraham fell into a deep sleep, and then it happened—a smoking firepot with a blazing torch appeared and passed between the pieces of the animals. Do you know what this means?"

The children all shook their heads. "I don't have a clue," admitted Daniel.

Sir John explained, "The smoking firepot with the blazing torch is a symbol for God's glorious presence."

"So it is a glory story!" declared Mary.

"That it is, lassie. Actually, every story in the Bible shows us God's glory. This is one of my favorite glory stories because God was telling Abraham, and us, that we can be sure He will keep His covenant promise. In those days when two people entered into a covenant, or an agreement, with each other, they would cut animals in two, and both people would walk between them. This showed that both of them were responsible to keep the covenant promise they made to each other. But Abraham did not walk between the pieces of the animals. Rather, God's presence passed between them. God was showing Abraham that He, the Lord, would do everything, and Abraham could do nothing. It all depended on God. It was a covenant of grace."

Sir John was quiet, and the children thought about what he had said. Then he continued, "There is a second thing that God was teaching Abraham."

"And us," added Cassie.

Sir John smiled. "Yes, lassie, and us. Cutting the animals in half meant that if the person who passed between the animals broke the covenant, he deserved to be punished, just like the animals. When God passed through, He was explaining that He would destroy Himself if He did not keep the promise. Now Abraham could be sure. Abraham knew that he couldn't trust himself, but he knew that he could trust God. God was bound by His own word to keep the promise. He kept that promise when Jesus came into the world to die for His people. Now, my young detectives, our treasure of wisdom and knowledge is in the very first verse of Genesis 15. What do we learn about God?"

"I see it!" proclaimed Angus. "God is our shield and very great reward."

"Very good," said Sir John. "This means that God will always protect us, He will always be with us, and He is everything we need. He is able to keep all of His promises to us."

"That was a great glory story," remarked Mary. And everyone agreed.

───────■───────

LET'S TALK

When God made the covenant promise to Abraham, what was the problem?

God promised that Abraham's children would be as many as what?

Who are Abraham's children?

What did God do so that Abraham would really know that He would keep the promise?

What did the smoking firepot and the blazing torch stand for?

What is the treasure of wisdom and knowledge?

Let's memorize God's Word: Proverbs 3:5-6.

───────■───────

LET'S PRAY

Thank God that He is your shield and very great reward.

CHAPTER TWENTY-SIX

The Beach Trip

TREASURE OF WISDOM AND KNOWLEDGE: God is our shield and reward.
COVENANT VALUE: Trust

Trust in the LORD with all your heart, and do not lean on your own understanding.
In all your ways acknowledge him, and he will make straight your paths.
(Proverbs 3:5-6)

"What is that?" asked Mac as they all turned to look at the huge motor home coming down the street.

Suddenly Cassie recognized the driver. "That's Mimi and Pop!" she exclaimed.

The children waved wildly as the enormous coach slowly approached. Pop knew he had an audience, and he was still trying to learn how to drive his new vehicle. He finally maneuvered the motor home into the driveway and parked it safely. Pop and Mimi climbed out and hugged all the children.

"Can we look inside?" asked Daniel.

"Yes, sirree." Pop smiled. He loved showing his new motor home to anyone who would look. "We've got a sink over here, and this folds out into a bed, and right over here—"

"Look at this!" interrupted Caleb. "Check out the size of this TV."

"Pop," scolded Mimi playfully, "I told you that television was too big." She always thought Pop spent too much money on his "toys."

"Okay, kids," called Mimi. "Everyone find a seat. We have an announcement."

Cassie and Caleb knew their grandmother was excited because her voice was squeaky—just like Cassie's excited voice, except that Mimi's voice was old. Cassie, Caleb, Mac, Mary, and Daniel scrambled around and found seats.

"Count and be sure they're all here before we tell them," ordered Pop.

Mimi did a quick head count and then said, "Five—three boys and two girls. All here. Tell them, Pop."

"No, sweetie, you tell them," he insisted.

Cassie smiled. *I love the way Pop calls her Sweetie*, she thought. *They may be old, but everyone knows they still love each other.*

"Somebody tell us!" begged several of the children at the same time.

"Well," began Mimi, "when we decided to buy a motor home, we thought and thought about where we would go on our first trip. Should we take a long trip or a short trip? Should we go to the mountains or the beach?"

"And we talked and talked about who we would take with us," continued Pop.

"We thought about some friends, and then we thought about some other friends," added Mimi.

"We decided most of our friends are too old," laughed Pop.

The children laughed as Mimi and Pop both tried to talk at the same time.

"Finally we decided," declared Pop.

"We're going to the beach, and we're taking all of you," announced Mimi.

"What?" exclaimed five voices. Then all of the children started talking at once.

"When are we leaving?"

"Do you think our parents will let us go?"

"How long are we staying?"

"What do we need to take?"

"Quiet!" laughed Pop. "We've already talked to your parents. We leave at 8:00 tomorrow morning."

"And be sure to bring your journals. We want you to tell us about the things you've been learning at Sir John's," requested Mimi.

When everyone gathered the next morning, the parents gave last-minute instructions.

"Be sure to put on plenty of sun screen."

"You do exactly what Mimi and Pop tell you to do."

"Remember your manners."

"Put your dirty clothes in the plastic bag."

There were lots of hugs and good-byes, and then they boarded and buckled up. As they drove off, Mimi looked at Pop and said softly, "I hope we haven't bitten off more than we can chew."

"Nonsense," returned Pop. But to tell the truth, he was a bit nervous as well. *Maybe we should have taken some of our old friends*, he thought to himself as he listened to five children talking at once.

They had not been driving long when a small voice said, "I have to go to the bathroom!"

"Me too!" came another voice.

"How long before we get there?" asked another child.

Finally they rolled into the campground. Soon they were on the beach, playing in the shallow waves and building sandcastles. Mimi and Pop relaxed in their beach chairs. They heard Caleb say, "This is the best," as he filled his bucket with more sand. And they heard Daniel respond, "Better than the best."

"I think we made a good decision," remarked Pop.

Later while Mimi and Pop cooked hamburgers and hotdogs, Pop said, "Mimi and I would like you to tell us what you've been learning this summer."

"We've been discovering treasures of wisdom and knowledge about God," Caleb responded. "Sir John says that the more we know about God, the more we'll become like Him."

"And we've been learning about connections," said Cassie. "Sir John gets really excited when we see how one part of the Bible is connected to other parts."

"Don't forget our covenant values," added Daniel.

"Whoa!" laughed Pop. "You kids have my old head spinning. Start over and explain it to us slowly. Caleb, take charge!"

Caleb loved being in charge. He opened his journal. "First, we learned that God is our glorious Creator. Mary, what is our covenant value? What should we do because God is our glorious Creator?"

"Reflect His glory," answered Mary.

Caleb continued, "And since God is the King of creation, what should His covenant people do, Mac?"

"We should be good stewards of everything God gives us," replied Mac.

"And since God is the God of grace, what should we do?"

"We should worship Him," answered Daniel.

By this time Caleb was quite full of himself, and he went a little overboard. "Splendid, splendid, splendid," he said.

All the kids just looked at him and then burst into laughter.

"Okay, I guess I got carried away," Caleb admitted. "Anyway, then we learned that God is a covenant keeper."

"And our covenant value is obedience," said Mac.

"And finally," said Caleb, "we learned that God is our shield and reward. Now we need to look up the clues to find the covenant value. Who'll read the first clue?"

"I will," offered Mary. She read Proverbs 3:5-6: "'Trust in the LORD with all your heart, and do not lean on your own understanding. In all your ways acknowledge him, and he will make straight your paths.'"

"The next clue is Psalm 20:7. Who wants to read it?"

"I will," said Mac. "'Some trust in chariots and some in horses, but we trust in the name of the LORD our God.'"

"Now the last clue is Psalm 56:3. Cassie, do you want to read this one?"

Cassie read: "'When I am afraid, I put my trust in you.'"

Caleb remembered something he had heard his dad say many times, and this seemed like the perfect time to repeat it. "That verse is just like you, Cassie—short and sweet."

"Oh, give me a break," Cassie groaned.

"I think I know what the covenant value is!" Mary exclaimed.

"Me too!" Cassie squealed.

Five voices shouted together, "It's trust!"

And Daniel, the charmer, never at a loss for words, looked at Mimi and Pop. "And I trust that those are the best hamburgers and hotdogs in the whole world!"

LET'S TALK

Since God is our glorious Creator, what should His children do?

Since God is the King of creation, what is a covenant value for His children?

Since God is the God of grace, what should His children do?

Since God is the covenant keeper, what should His children do?

Since God is our shield and reward, what should His children do?

Let's memorize God's Word: Proverbs 3:5-6.

LET'S PRAY

Ask the Lord to give you grace to trust Him with all your heart.

CHAPTER TWENTY-SEVEN

The Sea Creatures

TREASURE OF WISDOM AND KNOWLEDGE: God is our shield and reward.
COVENANT VALUE: Trust

*Trust in the LORD with all your heart, and do not lean on your own understanding.
In all your ways acknowledge him, and he will make straight your paths.
(Proverbs 3:5-6)*

———————————■———————————

"Well, breakfast in a motor home is really cool," declared Daniel.

"And loud!" said Pop as he gave orders to everyone about their clean-up chores. "As soon as you finish, let's gather around the picnic table outside for devotions. Bring your journals and your Bibles."

Soon everyone was settled, and Pop began. "I'm glad you children are thinking about trust. Mimi and I have learned that we can always trust God. To trust Him means that we put our hope that we will go to heaven in what Jesus did for us on the cross. We're safe with Him. God is trustworthy, and we can expect Him to take care of us and help us. Listen to these verses from Psalm 4."

Pop opened his Bible and read: "'. . . Put your trust in the LORD. . . . In peace I will both lie down and sleep; for you alone, O LORD, make me dwell in safety'" (vv. 5, 8). Then Pop prayed and asked the Lord to keep them safe as they played on the beach, and he prayed that all of the children would always trust God with all their hearts and never lean on their own understanding.

As soon as he said, "Amen," the children shouted, "Let's go to the beach!"

"Hold on," instructed Mimi. "Pop has a present for you."

"Okay, I have a kite for each one. I love flying kites here, and I know you will too."

Soon everyone was loaded down with beach stuff. As they walked, Pop said, "Let's go over our safety rules. When I blow my whistle, you must come instantly. You can only go in the water if I'm standing on the edge watching you. You must all stay where we can see you. And watch out for the sea creatures. This is the time of year when there are lots of jellyfish on the beach, and these peculiar-looking fish have tentacles that sting."

"We'll be careful!" they all promised, and off they ran to the water.

Pop and Mimi laughed as they watched the kids run away from the waves crashing on the beach. The girls squealed as Caleb chased them with a crab.

"Hey, let's fly the kites now," suggested Mac.

Pop helped them get the kites ready, and off they ran. "Where do they get all that energy?" he asked Mimi.

Pop chuckled as he got his own kite ready. It was huge. He knew the children would love it.

"Do you think your old legs will run fast enough to get that kite in the air?" asked Mimi.

"Just watch me," bragged Pop. As he ran down the beach, he saw that Daniel had turned around and was running toward him. Suddenly Pop yelled, "Daniel, stop! Trust me—don't move!"

Daniel was running in the edge of the water, but he instantly obeyed Pop even though it meant that his kite crashed to the ground. Pop carefully walked over and picked Daniel up. As Daniel looked down, he realized that he had been surrounded by jellyfish.

All the other children came running up to them. Pop pointed to the jellyfish. "Daniel, I'm glad you trusted me and immediately obeyed. That could have been big trouble."

"Umm," said Mac. "I think I see a connection with our devotion this morning." Everyone agreed.

That night after dinner Mimi and Pop suggested that they go for a walk on the beach. It was just beginning to get dark. When they came back, Mimi spread blankets out, and everyone lay down. They listened to the gentle sound of the ocean.

"Ah, this is nice," sighed Pop.

"Look at the stars!" Mac exclaimed. "I don't think I've ever seen so many."

"You know what all those stars remind me of?" Mimi asked.

"Space Mountain at Disney World!" Daniel yelled excitedly.

"No, not Space Mountain," laughed Mimi. "They remind me of Abraham."

"Oh, yeah—Abraham," mused Cassie. "God told Abraham that he would have as many children as there were stars in the sky."

"Right," replied Mimi. "Abraham trusted God, and God kept His promise. We can always trust God to keep every promise."

"It's good to know that we can always trust God, because there're *some* people around here that we *can't* trust," teased Mary.

"Like who?" Pop asked.

"Like . . . Cassie!" Mary pretended to be mad.

"Me?" Cassie was startled. "You can trust me!"

"What about this afternoon when you buried me in the sand?" asked Mary.

"Oh . . . that . . . I guess you have a point," laughed Cassie.

Mary turned to the others. "Cassie begged and begged me to let her bury me in the sand. She kept saying, 'You can trust me.' So I did. *Huge* mistake!"

"It was great," added Cassie. "She was completely covered except her head and feet." Cassie started giggling just thinking about the sight.

"There I was, absolutely helpless, and she tickled my feet with a seagull feather."

"I just couldn't help it," squealed Cassie. "It was hilarious!"

"Like this?" asked Mimi, and she and Mary began tickling Cassie unmercifully.

You can probably imagine how this ended—one tremendous tickling tirade under the twinkling stars.

LET'S TALK

When Daniel was flying his kite, why did Pop tell him to stop?

Did Daniel understand why Pop told him that?

What did Daniel do when Pop told him to stop?

What would have happened to Daniel if he had not trusted Pop?

What does this teach you about trusting and obeying God?

Look at Proverbs 3:5-6. What are two things this verse tells us to do?

What does Proverbs 3:5-6 tell us not to do?

How do we lean on our own understanding?

Let's memorize God's Word: Proverbs 3:5-6.

LET'S PRAY

Thank God that He is your shield and very great reward.

Ask Him to help you trust Him and obey Him.

CHAPTER TWENTY-EIGHT

The Rascal

TREASURE OF WISDOM AND KNOWLEDGE: God is our shield and reward.

COVENANT VALUE: Trust

Trust in the LORD with all your heart, and do not lean on your own understanding. In all your ways acknowledge him, and he will make straight your paths. (Proverbs 3:5-6)

———■———

"Story time," announced Mimi as the children gathered around her. They had just roasted marshmallows on the beach, and the soft breeze made everyone feel relaxed.

"Tell us a story about when you were a little girl," begged Cassie as she cuddled next to Mimi.

Mimi smiled. "When I was a little girl, every Sunday I walked with my daddy to the little church on the corner. We went early because my daddy was the Sunday school superintendent. It was his duty to ring the church bell that hung in the steeple. He would carefully unwind the huge rope, pull it slowly, and then the deep, wonderful sound of the bell could be heard all over our small town."

Cassie grinned. "I love this story."

Mimi continued, "Sometimes my daddy let me ring the bell. It was exciting. I felt that I was on the edge of a daring adventure because I was just a bit afraid that the big rope would yank me up into the steeple. I guess my daddy knew what I was thinking because when he handed me the rope, he would cock one of his bushy eyebrows and look at me with his crooked little grin. My daddy was a rascal."

"Like Pop?" asked Caleb.

"You better watch it, boy," laughed Pop. "You'll be looking for another ride home!"

Mimi smiled and continued, "I loved to hear my daddy sing in church. To tell you the truth, he didn't sing particularly well, but he sang loudly and he sang happily. His very favorite hymn was—"

"'My hope is built on nothing less than Jesus' blood and righteousness,'" finished Cassie and Caleb. They had heard Mimi tell this story many times.

"Now tell the funny part," pleaded Caleb.

"One Sunday," Mimi mused, "excitement filled the air. It was Sunday school promotion day, and all of the children and adults met together in the sanctuary. I had on a new dress my mama had made me, and I wore my little white gloves. I was a prissy little girl. My younger brother Donald sat with me, and I felt very responsible. I also felt very proud, because my daddy was the Sunday school superintendent, and he was in charge. My daddy was talking when suddenly an *outrageous* thing happened! Before I could stop him, Donald stood up on the church pew and hollered in his loudest voice, 'Tom, Tom, the piper's son, stole a pig, and away he run!'"

The children exploded in laughter.

Mimi pretended to be annoyed. "I didn't think it was one bit funny. I taught him that nursery rhyme, but I never intended for him to think it was a sermon! I jerked him down as quickly as I could and put my white-gloved hand over his mouth. I was horrified."

The children were roaring uncontrollably. Daniel was lying flat on his back, so tickled he was kicking his legs.

Mimi acted as if she saw nothing funny about it. "Well," she said, "at least the people in my church were more polite than you children. They all hid their giggles, except one old man who let out a belly laugh as loud as Donald shouted. I was appalled."

"What did your daddy do?" asked Mac.

"I could not believe my eyes," answered Mimi. "His bushy eyebrow was cocked, and he had that crooked little grin. Why, it was as if he were saying, 'That boy's a chip off the old block.' Well, my daddy had that much right—my brother was a rascal."

"I love that story," declared Cassie.

"I know you do," replied Mimi. "And your mother loved it when she was a little girl. She called my daddy Pop, and he used to tell her that story. Daddy was a rascal, but he loved and trusted the Lord Jesus. One of his favorite Bible passages was Proverbs 3:5-6. He helped me memorize it when I was a little girl, and I helped my children memorize it. I'm so glad you children are learning it too. Let's say it together."

A chorus of young voices said, "'Trust in the LORD with all your heart, and do not lean on your own understanding. In all your ways acknowledge him, and he will make straight your paths.'"

The children looked at the twinkling stars and listened to the sound of the waves.

"Is your daddy in heaven now?" asked Mac.

"Yes," replied Mimi. "He got older, and I got older. One day when I was sitting beside his bed, he opened his eyes, pointed up, and said excitedly, 'Look!' I was startled. 'What?' I asked. He cocked his bushy eyebrow, gave that crooked little smile, and said tenderly, 'You can't see them.' Then he closed his eyes and slept. And soon he died."

"What did he see?" asked Mary.

"I couldn't see what my daddy saw, but I'm sure he saw the angels. And I wonder if he heard bells ringing to welcome him home. Children, I know my daddy is in heaven because he trusted Jesus. His hope was built on nothing less than Jesus' blood and righteousness. God was his shield, and his reward was great. He was not afraid to die because he knew he was safe with Jesus . . . even though he was a rascal."

Cassie snuggled close to Mimi. Cassie was just a little girl, but she knew when someone needed a hug, and her Mimi needed a hug. After a while Cassie said, "Mimi, will you tell us a story about Pop? Tell us the one about the Sunday school program."

"Oh, Cassie," Mimi said smiling, "I like that one too. Pop was just about five years old, and his Sunday school class was going to recite some Bible verses in church. The Sunday school teacher was a very prim and proper lady, and she had instructed the children to stand straight and still and to pronounce their words clearly. Exactly on cue, every child began reciting . . . *except* Pop. For some unknown reason, he took three steps forward, gave a huge smile, and stood on his head! The other children continued to recite, and the audience tried to ignore him. The Sunday school teacher was bewildered, and Pop's poor mother was upset.

"Now you need to know that he could stand on his head with great skill. The Sunday school teacher had said to stand straight and still. Well, Pop was as straight as a pencil, as still as a stick, and he pronounced every word precisely, but he was *upside down*! His mother became increasingly distressed. She was afraid that all of the blood would rush to his head, and he would die on the spot! Finally she could stand it no longer. She jumped up out of her pew, ran down the aisle, up on the stage, and turned him right side up. Pop never missed a word—he kept reciting verses with the other children. But you probably don't want to hear what happened to that little rascal when he got home."

LET'S TALK

What are some things you liked about this story?

Why was Mimi sure her daddy was in heaven?

What is the treasure of wisdom and knowledge in this story?

What is the covenant value?

What Bible passage did Pop teach Mimi when she was a little girl?

What do you learn from Proverbs 3:5-6?

Let's memorize God's Word: Proverbs 3:5-6.

LET'S PRAY

Thank God that He is your shield and that your reward is very great.
Ask Him to help you to trust Him with all your heart.

The Solid Rock

CHAPTER TWENTY-NINE

Glory Story—God Provides

GENESIS 21—22

TREASURE OF WISDOM AND KNOWLEDGE: God provides.

COVENANT VALUE: Thankfulness

Continue steadfastly in prayer, being watchful in it with thanksgiving.
(Colossians 4:2)

——————■——————

The children arrived at Sir John's and settled into their places. As Cassie scooted back in the big leather chair, she asked, "Do we get to hear a glory story today?"

"Ah, lassie, it's a *glorious* glory story." Sir John handed each of them a card with a Bible verse written on it. "Today we're going to hear a story about Abraham. The verses are clues from the New Testament to help you see that Abraham's story gives us understanding about what the promised Savior would do for His people."

Sir John continued, "We have seen that God promised Abraham that the Savior would come from his family. Abraham and Sarah were too old to have children, and so it seemed impossible for God to keep the promise. But God did keep the promise. God gave them a baby boy. They were so filled with joy that they named him Isaac, which means 'laughter.'"

Then Sir John asked Cassie to read her clue.

Cassie read Luke 2:8-11: "'And in the same region there were shepherds out in the field, keeping watch over their flock by night. And an angel of the Lord appeared to them, and the glory of the Lord shone around them, and they were filled with fear. And the angel said to them, "Fear not, for behold, I bring you good news of a great joy that will be for all the people. For unto you is born this day in the city of David a Savior, who is Christ the Lord."'"

Sir John explained, "Isaac's birth was a miracle that brought joy to Abraham and Sarah. This is a picture to teach us that the birth of Jesus was also a miracle that brought joy to the whole world. Now back to Abraham. Someone read Genesis 22:2."

"I've got it!" said Mac. He read, "'He said, "Take your son, your only son Isaac, whom you love, and go to the land of Moriah, and offer him there as a burnt offering on one of the mountains of which I shall tell you."'" Mac was shocked. "Does this mean that Abraham was to kill his only son?"

Sir John spoke softly. "Ah, lad, remember the clues. Who has Clue #2?"

"Oh, it's me," replied Mac. He read John 3:16: "'For God so loved the world, that he gave his only Son, that whoever believes in him should not perish but have eternal life.'" He looked up. "So this helps us understand what it was like for God to give Jesus to die for us. What did Abraham do?"

"Look at Genesis 22:3," replied Sir John.

Mac hunted for the verse. "Here it is," he said and read: "'So Abraham rose early in the morning, saddled his donkey, and took two of his young men with him, and his son Isaac. And he cut the wood for the burnt offering and arose and went to the place of which God had told him.'"

The children were quiet for a few moments, and then Caleb said, "Now that's what I call trusting and obeying."

"But remember, children," explained Sir John, "Abraham trusted and obeyed because He knew that God would keep His promise. We have to look at Clue #3 to really understand what Abraham was thinking."

"I've got that one," said Caleb. He read Hebrews 11:17, 19: "'By faith Abraham, when he was tested, offered up Isaac. . . . He considered that God was able even to raise him from the dead. . . .'"

"Now look back at Genesis 22:4 and

5. Put on your spiritual spyglasses and see if you can find a clue that tells us that Abraham believed that God would indeed spare Isaac. Daniel, read the verses for us."

Daniel read: "'On the third day Abraham lifted up his eyes and saw the place from afar. Then Abraham said to his young men, "Stay here with the donkey; I and the boy will go over there and worship and come again to you."'"

All the children tried to find the clue. Finally Cassie squealed in her squeaky voice, "I see it! I see it! Abraham told the servant that '*I and the boy* . . . will come again to you.' Is that it, Sir John?"

"Indeed it is, lassie. What a good detective you are." Sir John was so excited that the buttons were about to pop off his plaid vest. "There is something else tucked in these verses that teaches us about Jesus."

Again all the heads looked down as the children scanned the verses. Then Daniel said, "This is so cool. 'On the third day' reminds us that Jesus was raised from the dead on the third day."

Well, now the children were sure those buttons on Sir John's vest were going to pop off. "Splendid! Splendid! Splendid!" he said. "As Abraham and Isaac walked up the mountain, Isaac asked his father a question. Mary, read verses 7 and 8."

Mary read: "'Isaac said to his father Abraham, "My father . . . where is the lamb for a burnt offering?" Abraham said, "God will provide for himself the lamb for a burnt offering, my son."'"

"Umm," mused Caleb, "I wonder if Isaac was beginning to suspect something. Do you think he knew that he was the sacrifice?"

"Well, if he didn't know it then, he soon realized it," replied Sir John. "Read verses 9 and 10."

Caleb read: "'When they came to the place of which God had told him, Abraham built the altar there and laid the wood in order and bound Isaac his son and laid him on the altar, on top of the wood. Then Abraham reached out his hand and took the knife to slaughter his son.'"

Cassie asked what everyone else was thinking: "Why didn't Isaac run?"

"Yeah," agreed Daniel. "Abraham was old. He couldn't catch Isaac."

"I get it," said Caleb. "This is a picture of Jesus going to the cross willingly for us."

Sir John raised his hands in the air and gave a loud "Splendid!" and one of those buttons popped right off and flew across the desk and into Cassie's lap. The startled children were speechless, and then they burst out laughing. Then Sir John asked, "Who has Clue #4? This verse tells us what Jesus said when the soldiers came to arrest and crucify Him."

"I have it," said Daniel. He read Matthew 26:53: "'Do you think that I cannot appeal to my Father, and he will at once send me more than twelve legions of angels?'"

Sir John explained, "Jesus was stronger and more powerful than the soldiers, but he obeyed His Father and let them put Him on the cross. Now back to Abraham. Mac, will you read Genesis 22:11-14?"

Mac read: "'But the angel of the LORD called to him from heaven and said, "Abraham, Abraham!" And he said, "Here am I." He said, "Do not lay your hand on the boy or do anything to him, for now I know that you fear God, seeing you have not withheld your son, your only son, from me." And Abraham lifted up his eyes and looked, and behold, behind him was a ram, caught in a thicket by his horns. And Abraham went and took the ram and offered it up as a burnt offering instead of his son. So Abraham called the name of that place, "The LORD will provide"; as it is said to this day, "On the mount of the LORD it shall be provided."'"

"Who has Clue #5?" asked Sir John.

"I have it," replied Mary. She read John 1:29: "'The next day he saw Jesus coming toward him, and said, "Behold, the Lamb of God, who takes away the sin of the world!"'"

"Well," said Caleb, "I guess I've heard this story a zillion times since I was born, but I never saw all that. The ram died in Isaac's place just like Jesus died in our place."

"Connection alert!" exclaimed Daniel. "You remember Pastor Scotty's sermon about the time when Jesus showed the disciples that all the Old Testament is about Himself?"

"Yeah," said Mac. "And their hearts burned with love for Jesus."

"And they obeyed Him and went and told others that He was alive," added Cassie.

"Now that I've seen Jesus in this story, I understand how the disciples felt," declared Caleb.

Sir John threw his hands up in the air. Before he could say, "Splendid!" Daniel shouted, "Duck, everyone! Flying buttons!"

———■———

LET'S TALK

Did Abraham have to actually offer his son Isaac as a sacrifice?

What did God provide so that Abraham did not have to sacrifice Isaac?

Who did God provide as the Lamb to be sacrificed in your place?

What is the treasure of wisdom and knowledge in this story?

Let's memorize God's Word: Colossians 4:2.

———■———

LET'S PRAY

Thank God for providing Jesus to die in your place.

CHAPTER THIRTY

The Scary Movie

TREASURE OF WISDOM AND KNOWLEDGE: God provides.

COVENANT VALUE: Thankfulness

*Continue steadfastly in prayer, being watchful in it with thanksgiving.
(Colossians 4:2)*

———————■———————

Cassie hung up the phone and ran to her mom. "Mom, guess what? Alice just invited me to go see a movie tonight with some girls on my soccer team. Mom, please let me go!"

"Cassie, you know our rule about movies," answered Mom. "Your dad and I must check to be sure it's something appropriate for you to see. God's Word tells us that whether we eat or drink or whatever we do, we should do it for His glory. If a movie is dishonoring to the Lord, we can't let you go."

"I know," said Cassie slowly. "But everybody is going. I don't want to be different."

"But we are different, Cassie," explained her mom. "We belong to God. We are His people. We have a responsibility to glorify Him by being good stewards of our minds."

"I know," said Cassie again. "Trash in—trash out." She knew the rule, but she wasn't a bit happy about it.

Cassie and Caleb's mom and dad had thought long and hard about their rule concerning movies. They had decided that they had a responsibility to protect their children's minds. They knew that what children see and hear on TV and in movies stays in their minds and affects their actions. This is why they started saying, "Trash in—trash out."

It was getting harder to keep the rule. The children had to turn down several invitations because their parents did not think the movie was suitable. Mom and Dad had even wondered if they were being too strict, and they asked the Lord to give them wisdom. Soon they were convinced that they were doing the right thing.

Cassie's mom sat down at the computer. "Okay, Cassie, I'll check on this movie." She brought up a website for movie reviews.

"Hurry, Mom," Cassie pleaded. "What does it say?"

"Umm," said her mom. Cassie could tell by her mother's tone of voice that it wasn't good news. "I don't think this one is appropriate for little girls."

"Oh, mom, please!" begged Cassie. "All my friends are going!"

Cassie knew her parents would not accept this argument. They had told her many times that if all her friends were going to jump off a cliff, her parents still would not let her do it.

"Cassie," Mom said slowly in that tone Cassie knew she shouldn't argue with, "this is a scary movie, and there is bad language in it. I love you, and I must protect you." Deep down Cassie knew her mom was right, but she was so disappointed.

That night Cassie was still sulking during devotion time. "Okay, kids," said their dad, "let's look at your journals. What is the treasure of wisdom and knowledge that you learned this week?"

"God provides," said Caleb. Then he explained, "God told Abraham to sacrifice Isaac, but at the last minute God provided a lamb instead. Now we need to find the covenant value." He opened his journal and read: "'How do you think Abraham felt when God provided the lamb to die in Isaac's place? Look up the clues to discover the answer.'"

Caleb read Clue #1: "(Psalm 100:4-5) 'Enter his gates with thanksgiving, and his courts with praise! Give thanks to him; bless his name! For the LORD is good; his steadfast love endures forever, and his faithfulness to all generations.'"

Mom read Clue #2: "(Colossians 3:15) 'And let the peace of Christ rule in your hearts, to which indeed you were called in one body. And be thankful.'"

Dad picked up his Bible and began to read Clue #3: "(Hebrews 12:28) 'Therefore let us be grateful for receiving a kingdom that cannot be shaken, and thus let us offer to God acceptable worship, with reverence and awe.'"

Then there was silence. "Cassie," said her dad, "will you read Clue #4?"

Cassie read, "(Colossians 4:2) 'Continue steadfastly in prayer, being watchful in it with thanksgiving.'"

Cassie was beginning to squirm. She knew she had not prayed and asked the Lord to help her to have an obedient attitude. She knew she wasn't thankful, and she suspected that she wasn't being watchful. She wanted to watch the movie, but she had an idea that that was not what the verse meant when it said to be watchful.

Dad continued, "Well, what do you think is the answer? How do you think Abraham felt when God provided the sacrifice?"

"I think he felt thankful," answered Caleb.

"Absolutely!" replied his dad. "Jesus is called the Lamb of God. He is the Lamb that God provided to die in our place. So how should we feel?"

"Thankful!" answered Caleb.

"Now let's read the memory verse for this covenant value," instructed their dad. They all read Colossians 4:2 together: "'Continue steadfastly in prayer, being watchful in it with thanksgiving.'"

Their dad explained, "When we devote ourselves to prayer, we will remember that God provided Jesus to die in our place, and that will make us thankful. Why should we be watchful? What should we watch for?"

"Well," said Cassie slowly, "we should watch out for things that will tempt us to sin—like movies that aren't good for us. Mom, I know you're watching out for me when you won't let me go to a movie. I'm sorry I was mad at you."

Cassie's mom and dad were grinning from ear to ear. "Cassie," said her dad, "it's because we're God's people that I can't let you do things that I don't think will honor Him. It's because He loves us so much that I must protect your mind."

"I know, Dad," said Cassie.

The next day at soccer practice Cassie's friend Alice, who had invited her to the movie, kept missing the ball. Finally Alice said, "I'm so tired I don't think I can run or dribble or anything."

"Why are you so tired?"

Alice replied, "That movie I saw last night was so scary I had bad dreams all night. You'd better be glad you didn't go, Cassie."

On the way home Cassie told her mother, "Mom, I have something else I'm thankful for."

"What's that, Cassie?"

"I'm thankful that God has given me Christian parents who love me so much that they protect me even when I give them a hard time."

LET'S TALK

What did Cassie want to do?

Why didn't her parents let her go?

Why was Cassie thankful that her parents didn't let her go?

How can we be watchful?

What is the treasure of wisdom and knowledge in this story?

What is the covenant value?

Let's memorize God's Word: Colossians 4:2.

LET'S PRAY

Thank God for providing Jesus to die for your sins in your place.

CHAPTER THIRTY-ONE

Changed Plans and a Changed Heart

TREASURE OF WISDOM AND KNOWLEDGE: God provides.

COVENANT VALUE: Thankfulness

Continue steadfastly in prayer, being watchful in it with thanksgiving.
(Colossians 4:2)

———————◼———————

Caleb woke up early. He was excited. Today he, Daniel, Mac, and Angus were going to build a fort in the woods behind Granny Grace's house. They were also going to look for treasures in the little creek. They had heard that someone once found a real Indian arrowhead there, and the boys were sure there were more to be found. They had decided to keep it a secret because it was going to be a boys' day with no girls allowed.

When Caleb went outside, Daniel and Angus were waiting for him.

"Are you ready?" Daniel asked.

"Oh yeah, I'm ready," Caleb answered excitedly.

"I'll bet we're millionaires by the end of the day," Daniel dreamed.

"Yeah, they'll be calling us heroes for all the important stuff we find," Caleb agreed.

As the boys got on their bikes, Cassie walked outside. "What're you doing today? Can I play?"

"No way," Caleb replied. "No girls allowed today."

Just then Caleb and Cassie's mom called, "Cassie and Caleb, come inside. I need to talk to you."

"But, Mom . . ." returned Caleb. He reluctantly put his bike down and ran inside.

"Jennifer's baby is sick, and she needs to take him to the doctor. She's bringing her twins over for me to watch. I need you both to help me."

Cassie and Caleb loved the twins, but the three-year-olds were like a tornado in their house! Cassie and Caleb knew that if they didn't watch them every minute, the twins would get into all their stuff.

"Good!" said Cassie. "I love playing with the twins."

"Aw, Mom!" Caleb protested. "Not today! I've got special plans!"

"Caleb, sometimes we change our plans to help others. The twins love for you to play with them, and it will be much easier if you and Cassie are here."

Caleb's day was ruined. What was going to be an incredible time of adventure was now going to be a boring day with his sister and two babies.

Later that day Daniel stopped by to show Caleb the treasures they had found. It wasn't exactly the stuff millionaires are made of, but it was a bucketful of interesting old trinkets. "And I've been stuck here with Cassie and the twins," Caleb grumbled.

At dinner their dad asked Cassie and Caleb about their day. "I missed a whole day of fun because we had to help take care of the twins. It just doesn't seem right," Caleb complained.

Mom and Dad looked at each other. Sometimes they knew what the other was thinking without anybody saying a word. They both knew they needed to pray for Caleb before they talked with him. After dinner they went to their room and prayed. Then they looked for Caleb. They went to his room and were surprised to see him lying on his bed crying.

"What's wrong?" they asked.

Caleb looked up. "I'm such a sinner," he said simply.

His parents looked at each other. "Tell us more, Caleb," his dad insisted.

"I've been so mean. I must not even be a Christian! I didn't care about the baby being sick. I didn't care about the twins. I just cared about myself," he said.

"Caleb, the Lord will forgive you.

You're His child. He provided Jesus to pay for your sins. You just need to repent and ask Him to forgive you."

"But I'm so bad," Caleb persisted. "It's not just today. I've been mean to Cassie all week. I didn't want her to play with us today because I didn't want her to have fun."

"Caleb, your heart has gotten dirty," his mom explained.

"How do I get it clean?" Caleb asked.

Caleb's mom picked up his Bible from his desk and read 1 John 1:9: "'If we confess our sins, he is faithful and just to forgive us our sins and to cleanse us from all unrighteousness.'"

Then his dad took the Bible. "Caleb, listen to this prayer from God's Word. I pray this every day." He opened the Bible and read Psalm 51:10: "'Create in me a clean heart, O God, and renew a right spirit within me.'"

"Caleb," his dad explained, "we're God's people. He loves us so much that when we tell Him we're sorry, He forgives us. He's so powerful that He can change our attitudes. We can ask Him to keep our hearts clean. He gives us grace so that we want to do what's right—even to change our plans. Let's pray right now."

They all knelt around Caleb's bed and prayed. When they finished, Caleb's dad got a piece of paper from Caleb's desk and wrote something on it. As he handed it to Caleb, he said, "When you're tempted to have a bad attitude or to be mean to Cassie, or any other temptation, I want you to come up here to your room and read this verse."

Caleb took the piece of paper and read, "'Little children, you are from God and have overcome them, for he who is in you is greater than he who is in the world'"(1 John 4:4).

His dad continued, "God has provided His Holy Spirit to live in you, Caleb, and He is more powerful than Satan."

"Umm," said Caleb. "I think I have a plan. Every time I want to be mean to Cassie or disobey you and Mom, I'll come up here and read this verse. Then I'll tell Satan to leave me alone because God is bigger than he is." Caleb thought for a few minutes and then said, "I sure am thankful that God lives in me."

"I am too," said Dad.

LET'S TALK

What happened to change Caleb's plans?

Was Caleb thankful that he could help take care of the twins?

What happened to change Caleb's heart?

What was Caleb's plan for times when he is tempted to disobey God?

Who has God provided to give us the power to obey Him?

Let's memorize God's Word: Colossians 4:2.

LET'S PRAY

Thank God for providing Jesus to die in your place
and thank Him that His Holy Spirit lives in you.

CHAPTER THIRTY-TWO

The Hike

Treasure of wisdom and knowledge: God Provides
Covenant Value: Thankfulness

Continue steadfastly in prayer, being watchful in it with thanksgiving.
(Colossians 4:2)

———◼———

The day did not start well for Cassie. She tended to be pokey in the mornings. Actually she was pokey most of the time.

"Hurry, Cassie," called her mom. "We told everyone to be ready at 9:00. It's very inconsiderate to be late."

They had invited Mary, Mac, and Daniel to go to a nature trail to hike and have a picnic. Cassie decided she *had* to take her doll, Miss Molly. Now Cassie was especially pokey when she took Miss Molly with her because she always had to bring some of Miss Molly's stuff. Gathering it all and putting it in the backpack took forever.

"Come on, Cassie. Everyone else is already in the car," called her mom.

"I can't decide what Miss Molly should wear," moaned Cassie.

"Then you'll just have to leave Miss Molly," said her mother firmly.

"Leave Miss Molly? But I promised her she can go." Cassie grabbed some doll clothes, stuffed them in her backpack, and rushed to the car.

When she climbed into the van, things did not get better. "It's about time!" growled Caleb. "We've been waiting for you."

The hike also was frustrating for Cassie. She insisted on carrying Miss Molly even though her mother warned her that she would get tired with the extra weight. As usual, her mother was right. "Let's go back. I'm tired," whined Cassie.

"Cassie, we all agreed that we would hike to the waterfall and have our picnic there," Mom reminded her.

"But I don't want to walk anymore," complained Cassie.

"Let's take a break," said her mom. "I need to check the map." While everyone rested, Caleb and his mom carefully looked at the map. "We really need to be watchful so we don't get on the wrong path," she said.

"Umm," said Caleb. "That makes me think about our memory verse: 'Continue steadfastly in prayer, being watchful in it with thanksgiving.'"

Cassie pretended she didn't hear. She knew she wasn't thankful, and it annoyed her to hear Caleb say the verse.

"Okay, time to move on," called Mom.

"I have an idea. Let's pretend we're covenanters on our way to a secret place to meet," suggested Caleb.

"Yeah!" exclaimed Daniel. "Everyone watch for the king's soldiers."

Mom joined in the game. "Why are you covenanters willing to risk your lives to go and worship together?" she asked.

"'For Christ's Crown and Covenant!'" shouted all the children triumphantly.

Well, all the children except Cassie. "I'm hot," she complained.

When they finally got to the waterfall, Cassie plopped down on the grass. Everyone else helped get the picnic ready. "Come on, Cassie, let's eat," said her mom.

Cassie slowly got up and walked to the blanket her mom had spread on the ground, but there was no place for her to sit. "Here's a towel, Cassie. You can sit on this," said her mom as she put the towel next to the blanket.

Well, that did it for Cassie. She lost it! "I don't want to sit on the towel. I want to sit on the blanket. This has been a terrible day. I just won't eat," she wailed as she walked over to a rock and sat down and sobbed.

Cassie's mother prayed in her heart, *Father, give me wisdom. I'm tired, and I don't want to deal with Cassie. Please give me grace to teach her to look to You for grace to have a thankful attitude.*

Everyone quietly ate lunch. Cassie's grumpiness made it seem as if a dark cloud hung over them. When they finished, the children went to the edge of the stream to play. Cassie's mom walked over and sat beside Cassie. "I saved you a piece of cake. You may have it after you eat your lunch." Cassie didn't say anything. "Cassie, your behavior has been bad, but I don't want to just talk about how you acted. I'm concerned about your heart. I know you're miserable, and you aren't going to feel better until you talk to the Lord. You feel terrible because you whined and complained. You do not have a thankful attitude. You need to ask the Lord to forgive you. Would you like to do that?"

Cassie shook her head.

"I understand," said her mom. "When I have a sinful attitude, I don't want to pray either. So I'm going to pray that God will give you grace to want to confess your sin." Her mom prayed. They sat in silence.

After a while Cassie began praying, "Dear Jesus, I'm sorry I've complained. Please forgive me."

Cassie's mom put her arm around her. "Cassie, you're God's child. He always forgives you when you ask Him. How do you feel now?"

"I'm tired," sighed Cassie.

"I understand that too, Cassie. Sin makes us very tired. A complaining attitude takes away our energy, but a grateful heart makes us joyful. Why don't we think of some things we're thankful for."

Cassie thought for a minute. "Well, I guess I'm thankful for legs so that I could go on this hike."

Her mom laughed. "I'm thankful for this beautiful place where I can spend the day with my little girl and her friends."

"And I'm glad I have friends—even though I haven't been too nice to them today," said Cassie. She was beginning to perk up a bit, and so she kept going. "And I'm thankful that Jesus forgives me when I sin."

Her mom tousled her hair. "Are you ready for your lunch now?"

Cassie ate her peanut butter and jelly sandwich and was finishing the last bite of cake when Mary ran up. "Will you come play with us, Cassie?"

"Sure." Cassie jumped up and ran off. But then she stopped and ran back to her mom. "There's something else I'm thankful for," she said.

"What?" asked her mom.

"A mom who saves me a piece of cake." Cassie smiled.

LET'S TALK

Why did the day start badly for Cassie?

How does whining and complaining make us feel?

How did Cassie's grumpiness make everyone else feel?

*A map helps us to stay on the right hiking trail.
What are some things we should watch for if we want
to stay on the path of obedience?*

Did Cassie want to ask God to forgive her?

What did her mother pray?

After Cassie asked God to forgive her, what did she and her mother do?

Let's memorize God's Word: Colossians 4:2.

LET'S PRAY

Ask God to help you to be watchful and to have a thankful heart.

CHAPTER THIRTY-THREE

Glory Story— God's Sovereign Love

GENESIS 37—50

TREASURE OF WISDOM AND KNOWLEDGE: God is sovereign.
COVENANT VALUE: Love

A new commandment I give to you, that you love one another: just as I have loved you, you also are to love one another. (John 13:34)

———■———

After dinner Sir John went to his library and prayed. He got up early the next morning and prayed. At breakfast he said to Miss Jenny, "I've been praying for the children. I want them to understand the story for today."

"Is it a glory story?" she asked with an impish grin. They both enjoyed the way the children always asked that question.

The old gentleman smiled. "Indeed it is. I want the children to discover the treasures. I want them to understand that this story is about God's glorious, sovereign love for His children."

"Then I will pray with you, Papa," offered Miss Jenny.

From the moment the children arrived, Sir John knew that something was wrong. It did not take long to discover the problem. The children had quarreled. It had all started when Caleb said he had a great plan for the afternoon. Caleb had become a little boastful recently, and this time it angered Mac. "You always want to be in charge," he accused.

Mary immediately sided with her brother and added, "Yeah, you and Cassie always want to boss everyone else."

"What do you mean?" demanded Cassie.

It was not a happy walk, and it was not a happy group sitting in Sir John's library. Sir John knew that the story he was about to tell the children was exactly the story they needed to hear. He prayed that the Lord would make their hearts tender. "This will be our last story from Genesis. The treasure of wisdom and knowledge in this story is that God is sovereign."

"Sovereign? Isn't that like a king?" asked Mac.

"Very good, laddie . . . thus, the crown!" Sir John grinned and held up a paper crown. "Okay, I know it leaves something to be desired, but you get the idea. A sovereign is a king. The Bible teaches us that God is sovereign. That means that He is powerful, and He is in complete control of all things. There are three things about God's sovereignty that I want you to discover. Listen carefully. You have probably heard the story of Joseph."

"I have," said Daniel. "He's the guy whose daddy gave him the coat of many colors, and all his brothers were jealous of him."

Sir John nodded. "Joseph had a dream that his family was gathering grain, and everyone's bundle bowed down to his bundle. Joseph proudly told his family about his dream—"

"And his brothers got mad!" interrupted Daniel.

"Indeed they did," continued Sir John. "Their jealousy turned into hatred, and they sold Joseph to some travelers who took him to Egypt. Joseph and his brothers were the great-grandsons of Abraham. God had promised that the Savior would come from this family. What a dreadful thing to happen. The unity of the covenant family was broken, but they were still the covenant family. Here is the first treasure."

Sir John handed Cassie another crown with some words written on it. She read: "'We are God's covenant children because of His sovereign love.'"

"Sovereign love?" asked Mac. "What does that mean?"

Sir John explained, "God is the sovereign King. He sovereignly decides who will be His children. Joseph and his brothers did not earn God's love, and neither do we. It is free, sovereign love."

"What happened to Joseph?" asked Mary.

"Good question, lassie. Everyone turn to Genesis 39 and see if you can find the answer."

Everyone quickly turned the pages of their Bibles. "He was sold to a man named Potiphar," answered Mary.

"And the LORD was with Joseph," added Cassie.

"And Potiphar put Joseph in charge," said Mac.

"Very good, my young scholars. But then another terrible thing happened. Potiphar's wife lied about Joseph, and he was put in prison."

Caleb was looking at his Bible. "'But the LORD was with Joseph and showed him steadfast love and gave him favor in the sight of the keeper of the prison'" (Genesis 39:21).

Sir John smiled. "Here is the second treasure."

He handed another crown to Mary. She read: "'God can keep His promise to be with us always because He is sovereign.'"

Sir John explained, "God was in control of everything that happened to Joseph, even though there were times when it probably seemed that God had forgotten about him. Two men in the prison had dreams, and God told Joseph what the dreams meant. Joseph told one of the men that his dream meant that he would get out of prison and serve as the king's butler. The man forgot about Joseph until the king had a dream. Then the butler remembered. The king sent for Joseph and asked him if he could tell what the dream meant. Caleb, read Genesis 41:16 to see what Joseph told Pharaoh."

Caleb read: "'I cannot do it,' Joseph replied to Pharaoh, 'but God will give Pharaoh the answer he desires'" (NIV).

Sir John looked at the children. "Joseph's pride was gone. He had learned that he was not great or powerful. He could not interpret the dream, but God would tell him what it meant. Joseph told Pharaoh that there would be seven years of plenty and then seven years of famine. Pharaoh put Joseph in charge of everything he had. For seven years Joseph stored the extra grain so there would be food for the people when the famine came. One day Joseph's brothers came to buy grain for their family. They did not recognize Joseph. As Joseph listened to them, he realized that they were sorry for what they had done to him. When he finally told them who he was, they were terrified."

Mac was stunned. "What did Joseph do?"

"He was kind to his brothers, and he told them to bring all the family to Egypt, and he would care for them."

"That's amazing. Those brothers had been so mean to him," said Mac.

"Ah, lads and lassies, now it's time to discover the third treasure. Get your spiritual spyglasses on. Let's search. Why did Joseph forgive his brothers? What had he learned about God? Look at Genesis 50:19-21."

Mac read: "'But Joseph said to them, "Do not fear. . . . you meant evil against me, but God meant it for good, to bring it about that many people should be kept alive, as they are today. So do not fear; I will provide for you and your little ones." Thus he comforted them and spoke kindly to them.'"

Sir John handed Daniel another crown. Daniel read: "'God's covenant children can love one another because of God's sovereign love for us.'"

"Children, our covenant value is love. Joseph understood that everything that happened to him was God's plan. He could love and forgive his brothers because he knew that it was really God who had sovereignly planned out everything in his life. Now the family was united again. God wants His covenant children to love each other, but we can only do that when we understand His sovereign love for us. We'll be proud and selfish, and we'll be mean to each other until we understand God's sovereign love."

"Sir John, I've been acting like Joseph when he was proud," confessed Caleb.

"And I was acting like his brothers," admitted Mac.

"You've been acting the way we all act when we forget God's sovereign love for us," said Sir John. All the kids agreed, and then they told each other they were sorry.

"I think I understand how Joseph and his brothers felt when they made up," sighed Cassie.

"Yeah, I was miserable when we were fussing with each other," agreed Mary.

"God's sovereign love is a great treasure. Thanks for helping us find it, Sir John," said Caleb.

And then the happy group went to the kitchen to find shortbread.

LET'S TALK

Why were the children unhappy?

What is the treasure of wisdom and knowledge that we learn in this story?

What are three things the children learned about God's sovereignty?

What is the covenant value?

Let's memorize God's Word: John 13:34.

LET'S PRAY

Thank God for His sovereign love and ask Him to help you love others.

Mac Forgives

TREASURE OF WISDOM AND KNOWLEDGE: God is sovereign.

COVENANT VALUE: Love

A new commandment I give to you, that you love one another: just as I have loved you, you also are to love one another. (John 13:34)

———■———

Caleb was stretched out on the grass taking a break. "I love summer," he mused.

"Me too," agreed Angus.

"Me three," said Daniel. "I wish it was always summer."

It was an end-of-summer workday at the church, and the boys had been helping the men with out-side projects.

"I wonder how the girls are doing cleaning the nursery," said Caleb.

As soon as the words were out of his mouth, he heard his sister. "Has anyone seen Mary? We need her to help us," Cassie called from the nursery window.

Caleb looked at Angus and Daniel. "Yeah, I thought Mac and Mary were coming. I wonder where they are?" Then he answered his sister. "Sorry, Cassie, we haven't seen her."

The boys were back at work when Granny Grace's car pulled into the parking lot, and Mary and Mac got out.

"If you can't get here on time, just get here when you can," Caleb teased.

"Listen," Mac snapped, "we got here as soon as we could."

Caleb stared at his friend in surprise. It wasn't like Mac to get upset at a little friendly teasing. "Sorry, Mac. I was just playing. No big deal."

Cassie looked out the window, saw Mary and Mac, and called, "Hey, where've you been?"

"You people are really getting on my nerves," growled Mac. He shrugged and walked off. Mary smiled apologetically and went inside to join Cassie.

"I wonder why he's in such a huff," pondered Daniel.

"He must not want to spend the day working," responded Angus.

Caleb was sad that Mac didn't want to help clean the Lord's house. He started to say something, but then decided it would be best to keep quiet. What Caleb didn't know was that Mac's bad attitude had nothing to do with working at the church.

Angus called to Mac, "Hey, Mac, come on back and help us pick up trash."

"I hate being outside," Mac grumbled as he kept walking.

Pastor Scotty was nearby and heard everything. He waited a few minutes and then followed Mac to the back of the church. Mac was sitting on the steps. Pastor Scotty sat beside him. "Is there anything you'd like to talk about?" he asked.

That was all it took. Mac couldn't hold back the tears. Finally he blurted out, "I was excited all week. This was going to be the greatest day. I would be with the guys and work at the church. I've never done anything like this. Caleb told me that the boys help the men with projects. Then this afternoon Dad was coming to take Mary and me out for pizza and then to the go-cart rides. I could hardly wait.

"But this morning before I got out of bed, I heard the phone ring. I got up and went downstairs. I saw that it wasn't good news. Mom said that my dad isn't coming. Mary cried, but I just got really mad. I'm still mad, but also I'm sad."

Pastor Scotty put his arm around Mac. "I'm so sorry," he said. He hugged the little boy. Then he said, "Mac, people will disappoint us, but do you know who will never disappoint us?"

"G-God," Mac sobbed softly.

"That's right. I want you to listen very carefully.

Romans 8 says: 'And we know that for those who love God all things work together for good. . . . Who shall separate us from the love of Christ? Shall tribulation, or distress, or persecution, or famine, or nakedness, or danger, or sword? . . . For I am sure that neither death nor life, nor angels nor rulers, nor things present nor things to come, nor powers, nor height nor depth, nor anything else in all creation, will be able to separate us from the love of God in Christ Jesus our Lord'" (Romans 8:28, 35, 38-39).

They sat quietly a few moments, and then Pastor Scotty continued, "Mac, over and over in His Word God tells us that we are His people and that He lives with us. He will never leave us. I don't know why your dad didn't come. I don't know if there was some reason that he couldn't come. But I do know this: God has promised that nothing can separate us from His love. And He can keep that promise because He is sovereign."

Mac nodded. "Sir John told us that God is sovereign. Even when bad things happened to Joseph, God was in control of it all."

"Exactly!" said Pastor Scotty. "And do you remember what Joseph did to his brothers who had been so cruel to him?"

"He forgave them," sniffed Mac. "But I don't want to forgive Dad! I'm really mad at him."

Pastor Scotty looked Mac straight in the eye. "I understand that. I'm pretty mad at him right now too. So we need to pray about it."

Pastor Scotty thanked God for His love. He thanked God that nothing can separate us from that love. And He thanked God that even though we can't always understand it, He will use everything that happens to us for His glory. Then he asked the Lord to give Mac grace to forgive his dad. "And, Lord," prayed Pastor Scotty, "I need grace to forgive and love Mac's dad too."

When Pastor Scotty said, "amen," Mac began to pray. He asked the Lord to help him to forgive his dad. "And, Lord, thank You so much that You will never leave me," he prayed.

Pastor Scotty put his arm around Mac again. "You're a fine young man, Mac. I'm very thankful for God's grace in you. It takes a strong Christian to be willing to forgive someone who has hurt him."

Mac was encouraged. Pastor Scotty's words made him feel better. He stood up. "I think there's something else I need to do."

"What's that?" asked Pastor Scotty.

"I think I need to go ask the guys to forgive me. I was pretty rude to them. And I should go check on Mary. She was disappointed that Dad didn't come too."

Mac started to walk away, but he heard Pastor Scotty make a sniffing noise. He turned around and saw that Pastor Scotty was crying. "Are you okay?" he asked.

Pastor Scotty smiled. "These are tears of joy, Mac. When I see our covenant children loving others because they are learning how much God loves them, I see the power of the Gospel. It doesn't get any better than that!"

———■———

LET'S TALK

Why was Mac in such a bad mood?

Why do you think he took his anger out on his friends?

What are some things that Mac and Pastor Scotty talked about?

How did Mac show love for his dad?

How did he show his love for his friends?

How did he show his love for Mary?

Let's memorize God's Word: John 13:34.

———■———

LET'S PRAY

Thank God that He is sovereign and that He can keep His promise
never to leave us. Thank Him that nothing can separate us from His love.
Ask Him for grace to love others, even those who hurt us.

CHAPTER THIRTY-FIVE

Love Wins

TREASURE OF WISDOM AND KNOWLEDGE: God is sovereign.

COVENANT VALUE: Love

A new commandment I give to you, that you love one another: just as I have loved you, you also are to love one another. (John 13:34)

———————■———————

"I'm so excited and so nervous. . . . I can hardly wait until our first game. . . . Actually I can hardly wait until our first practice. . . . Look at my cleats, Cassie. Can you believe it? I'm going to be on a real soccer team! Do you think I'll ever learn how to kick this ball?"

Cassie loved seeing Mary so excited. All the kids had signed up for soccer, and it was Mary's first time to play on any kind of team. "Come on, Mary, let's go outside and practice. Caleb is setting up cones so we can practice dribbling around them."

The girls ran out to join the boys, who were already playing.

"Who wants to see if they can score on me?" Mac called as he set up two cones as a goal.

"I'm going to score thirty goals this season," Caleb bragged.

"Me too," Daniel proclaimed.

"All right, let's see if you can get past me." Mac crouched into a ready position.

"Well, I probably won't score any goals, but I sure am excited about playing." Mary laughed as she tried to dribble the ball. "This is harder than it looks," she called to Cassie.

Mary's mom walked outside and sat on the steps. She was happy to see Mary so excited. "Keep your eye on the ball, Mary," she coached.

Suddenly Caleb kicked a goal and let out a loud whoop. Mary looked up to see what the commotion was about, and her feet got tangled around the ball. She tripped and fell on her leg in a strange way. Mary screamed. Her mother immediately knew this was not just a simple fall. She jumped up and was instantly beside Mary, and so was Mac. All the kids gathered around.

"Is she hurt bad?" Mac asked.

"I think so. It's already starting to swell. We need to get her to the emergency room."

Caleb ran to get his parents. They were back in a flash. His dad gently lifted a sobbing Mary and took her to his car. Mary's mom was fighting back the tears as she got in the backseat with Mary.

"Don't worry about Granny Grace and Mac," Caleb's mom called to her. "I'll take care of everything."

Suddenly Mary's mom was thankful for these people who were so kind to her. *I'm glad I'm not alone,* she thought.

Granny Grace was at Miss Jenny's house, so they all went there to tell her what had happened. The children were pretty upset. Mary had looked so pitiful. Everyone gathered in Sir John's library. "Children," he said, "remember the treasures. Tell me some things you have learned about God that will comfort us right now."

Mac spoke first. "God is sovereign, and He can keep His promise to always be with us. I know He's with Mary right now."

Daniel added, "God is our shield and reward. I know that we can trust Him to take care of Mary."

Cassie's voice was filled with love as she said what everyone was thinking. "If Mary's leg is broken, she won't be able to play soccer. But I know that God is the glorious Creator and that we are His people. I think we should pray that Mary will glorify Him even if her leg is broken."

Sir John, Granny Grace, Miss Jenny,

and Cassie's mom were speechless. They were so thankful that the children had discovered such precious treasures.

"My dear children," said Sir John, "Cassie is right. Let's pray that Mary will remember the treasures. Let's ask God to give her grace to glorify Him and to be a good steward of this situation."

After a time of prayer, they piled into cars and went to the hospital. Pastor Scotty and his family and Hunter were already there. "Mary is having X-rays," they reported. Mary's mom looked frantic.

"Listen to this," said Pastor Scotty. "Dr. Ryan is on duty, and he's taking care of Mary." Dr. Ryan was a member of their church, and all the kids loved him.

"Really?" replied Cassie in delight. "I prayed that Dr. Ryan would be here and take care of her. Mary *loves* him. Thank You, Jesus! Thank You, Jesus!"

Daniel announced, "God provides!"

Mary's mom didn't say anything, but she was watching and listening. She had never seen so much love. Soon Dr. Ryan came out. When he saw the large crowd that had gathered, he smiled. "Well, the church has gathered. I knew God's people were praying. Our little Mary has such peace. She kept telling all the nurses and technicians that she was not afraid because Jesus is with her." Dr. Ryan looked at Mary's mom. "Her leg is broken. We're getting ready to put a cast on it. You can come back and see her before we get started." Then he looked at Pastor Scotty. "Why don't you come in and pray for Mary."

As they walked in, Mary's mom said, "She won't be able to play soccer, will she?"

"Not this season," Dr. Ryan replied.

"Does she know?"

"Yes." Dr. Ryan nodded. "But your little girl is trusting Jesus."

Mary's mom fought the tears when she walked into the room and saw Mary lying on the stretcher. "Oh, Mary, I'm so sorry," she said as she sat beside her. "And I'm so sorry you can't play soccer. It's just not fair. You want to play so badly."

"Mom, it's okay. God is in control." Mary even surprised herself that she was so calm about missing something she wanted to do so much.

"You mean you're not upset?" her mom questioned.

"I'm disappointed," Mary explained, "but I know God is sovereign. Sir John told us about Joseph. Bad things happened to him, but it was all part of God's plan. God loves me, and His plan for me is good."

Pastor Scotty quietly took Mary's hand, and the little group formed a circle. He thanked God for giving Mary the grace to trust and obey. He asked God to give Dr. Ryan wisdom as he cared for Mary. And he prayed that Mary's leg would heal quickly. Then he thanked God for loving us so much that He provided Jesus to die for our sins.

Dr. Ryan said, "Now we need to put the cast on Mary. Pastor Scotty, why don't you take Mary's mom back to the waiting area."

Mary's mom began to cry.

Mary smiled. "It's okay, Mom. I won't be alone. Jesus is my Savior. He loves me, and He'll be with me."

"Mary," said her mom softly, "I think I need to know this Jesus who loves you so much."

LET'S TALK

What happened to Mary?

When the children gathered in Sir John's library, what did he ask them to remember?

How do the treasures of wisdom and knowledge help us when there is a crisis?

What did the children pray that Mary would do?

How did the members of the church show love to Mary's mom?

How did the treasure of God's sovereignty help Mary?

Was Mary a good steward of this situation?

How did God use Mary's broken leg to do something wonderful?

How does it make you feel to know that God loves you and that He is sovereign?

Let's memorize God's Word: John 13:34.

LET'S PRAY

Thank God that He is sovereign and that He works everything out to accomplish His plan. Ask Him for grace to know Him better and to love Him more. Ask Him for grace to love others.

CHAPTER THIRTY-SIX

For Christ's Crown and Covenant

TREASURE OF WISDOM AND KNOWLEDGE: God is sovereign.

COVENANT VALUE: Love

A new commandment I give to you, that you love one another: just as I have loved you, you also are to love one another. (John 13:34)

When Pastor Scotty and Mary's mom walked out of Mary's hospital room, Mary's mother stopped and asked him, "May we talk?"

"Absolutely!" he said.

"I've been running away from God. I was angry and scared. I didn't believe He cared, and I didn't believe He would help me. But I've seen what a difference He has made in Mary and Mac. I've seen His love in all the people from church. I'm such a sinner. I need a Savior."

"Are you sorry for your sin, and do you want to turn away from it?" asked Pastor Scotty.

"Oh yes," she answered.

"Do you believe that when Jesus died on the cross, He did everything necessary to save you from your sin? Do you believe that His love for you is greater than you can imagine? Do you trust Him with all your heart?" continued Pastor Scotty.

"I do!" exclaimed Mary's mom.

"Would you like to let the others share in this moment?" asked Pastor Scotty.

"I would," she replied.

They walked to the waiting area. Pastor Scotty told the people gathered everything that had happened. The group of God's covenant people joined hands as Mary and Mac's mom prayed and asked Jesus to be her Savior.

"Just think," said Mac as he hugged his mom, "God used Mary's broken leg to help you become a Christian. He is so good and sooo sovereign."

"I have a great idea!" announced Miss Jenny.

"I know what you're thinking, Jenny," replied Granny Grace. "Let's go get ready." And the two friends scurried out.

"I may not be the smartest kid in the world," Daniel grinned, "but I'll bet that has something to do with shortbread and a party."

Cassie and Caleb's mom laughed. "I think you're exactly right. Come on, kids, let's go help!"

When the rest of the group arrived at Granny Grace's, there were balloons and a big banner that said, "Welcome Home!"

"Cool cast," said Mac when his sister emerged from the car.

As Cassie's dad carried Mary into the house, Pastor Scotty and his family arrived. "We've got the ice cream," called Angus.

"And lots of toppings," squealed Susie.

Mary sat in a chair with her leg propped on a stool and reigned over the event like a queen. Everyone was asking questions. Then Granny Grace took charge. "Quiet, everyone!" she called. "I'm so glad you're all here for this special occasion. Our "Welcome Home" banner has two meanings. Mary, we all welcome you back home. We're sorry about your broken leg, but we want you to know we love you."

Then Granny Grace looked at Mary's mom. "The second thing the banner means, my dear daughter, is that we welcome you to the family of God. You now have a home in heaven, and you have a covenant family here on earth. I thank God for answering my prayers."

Mary and Mac's mom looked so happy. She said, "You have all shown me the love of Jesus. I was listening to you even when you thought I wasn't interested. I've seen the power of God's grace in Mary and Mac, and after they went to sleep at night, I looked at their journals. I've been thinking about Christ's crown and covenant. Today I finally understood God's grace, and I realized that I want Jesus to be my King."

Then she looked at Granny Grace. "Mama, thank you for teaching me about Jesus when I was a little girl. I know that you never stopped asking God to give me a heart to know Him. Somehow even though I tried to run away from the Lord, I always knew that He was there. Now I understand that He was always with me because He set His affection on me, and He would not turn me loose. I'm so thankful that you and our church never stopped praying for me."

Then she looked at all the children. "Covenant children," she said. The children could feel her love for them and her desire to tell them something very important. They listened eagerly. "For many years I did not acknowledge God. I leaned on my own understanding. I did what I wanted to do, but it did not make me happy. I was miserable. Oh, children, trust Him with all your heart. Thank Him for your parents and your church family who teach you about Him. Pray for grace to glorify Him in everything you do. Keep searching for the treasures of wisdom and knowledge."

There were lots of happy tears and lots of hugs. Then Granny Grace said, "And now before we have refreshments, we'll have a signing ceremony!"

She held up colored markers and told everyone that they could sign Mary's cast. "Wait!" yelled Mary over the noise. "I want Sir John to sign my cast first, and I know exactly what I want him to write. On the front, where everyone can see it, I want him to write 'For Christ's Crown and Covenant.'

LET'S TALK:

What did you like about this story?

If someone asked you how to become a Christian, what would you tell the person?

What are some things you have learned about being a part of God's covenant family?

What are some of the privileges of being a part of God's covenant family?

What are some of the responsibilities of being a part of God's covenant family?

What are some of the treasures of wisdom and knowledge about God that you have discovered?

Let's memorize God's Word: John 13:34.

LET'S PRAY

Thank God for His covenant of grace.
Thank Him that He is the King of heaven and earth.
Ask Him for grace to know Him better and to love Him more.

Dear Covenant Child,

The real Cassie, Scotty, Hunter, Mary, Daniel, Susie, Mac, and Angus join us in praying that the Lord will use this book to help you know Him better. We pray that you and your family will continue to discover treasures of wisdom and knowledge in God's Word, and that His covenant values will become your values. And we pray that you will love and serve your covenant family. They are God's gift to you, and you are God's gift to them.

The cousins in our family ask you to join them in their cousin covenant:

"They entered into a covenant to seek the Lord, the God of their fathers, with all their heart and with all their soul." (2 Chronicles 15:12)

If you are not a covenant child, if you are not trusting Jesus as your Savior, we pray that you will turn from your sin and turn to Jesus.

In case you're wondering, there is not a real Caleb, but there is another cousin that we didn't put in this book. His name is Sam, and you just may see him in another covenant promises book. Stay tuned!

Susan Hunt and Richie Hunt

Parts of the Whole

J ust as we are each part of the whole family of Christ worldwide and throughout generations, so these books support and complement one another. Throughout each runs a theme of living covenantally—of seeing the wide expanse of God's mercy and grace to us intricately woven into every relationship and detail of life— and passing the legacy on to others.

Leaving a Legacy

Heirs of the Covenant—While today's broken culture grasps for direction, you can discover what happens when the church offers true Christian education and you fulfill your calling to leave a legacy of faith for the next generation. *Leader's Guide Available*.
TPB, ISBN 1-58134-011-7, $13.99

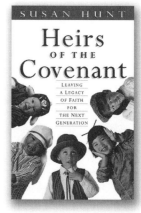

Fashion a Life Where God is Welcome

Your Home: A Place of Grace—Explore how covenant values help you fashion a life where God is welcome, a heart where He freely lives and a spiritual home that realizes the joy of His presence every day. *Leader's Guide Available*.
TPB, ISBN 1-58134-185-7, $12.99

Telling the Next Generation

Big Truths—Teach your kids the basics of the Christian faith with this fun, illustrated book. Its stories of everyday situations will help them integrate those truths in a way that finds expression at home, at school and with friends. Ages 3 to 8.
HC, ISBN 1-58134-106-7, $15.99

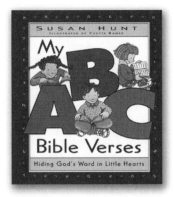

A Fun Way to Learn Biblical Values

My ABC Bible Verses—A colorful, story-filled way for even your youngest child to take God's Word to heart—and learn the alphabet too! It's a great resource for teaching biblical values to your kids at home, school or church. Ages 3-7.
HC, ISBN 1-58134-005-2, $14.99

For You as a Woman

By Design—A joyous celebration of God's "helper" design for women that will challenge you to explore the significance of your biblical calling and rally the church to equip one of its greatest resources: you.
TPB, ISBN 0-89107-976-9, $12.99

For Women Mentoring Women

Spiritual Mothering—This dynamic resource helps you find out why Paul's message in Titus 2 of older women "caring for" younger women is so important for you and how you can begin nurturing these important relationships.
TPB, ISBN 0-89107-719-7, $13.99

The Beauty and Strength of Godly Women

The True Woman—Set your heart on fire and get excited about the unique opportunity you have as a godly woman to make a difference for eternity as you discover how to reflect Christ in all areas of life.
TPB, ISBN 0-89107-927-0, $12.99